Also by Peter Matthiessen

TIGERS IN THE SNOW

Peter Matthiessen

TIGERS IN THE SNOW

INTRODUCTION & PHOTOGRAPHS

by

Maurice Hornocker

THE HARVILL PRESS
LONDON

First published in 2000 in the United States by North Point Press,
a division of Farrar, Straus and Giroux, New York

First published in Great Britain in 2000
by The Harvill Press
2 Aztec Row • Berners Road
London N1 0PW

www.harvill.com

1   3   5   7   9   8   6   4   2

Grateful acknowledgement is made to *The New Yorker* and *Audubon* magazine, in which some of the material in this book first appeared, in an altered form.

All tiger photographs are by Maurice Hornocker except for those on pp. 125 and 142, which are by Marc Moritsch, and p. 162, which is by Howard Quigley.

Art credits: p. 7, Hermitage Museum, St. Petersburg, photograph courtesy of CORBIS/Archivo Iconografico, S.A.; pp. 44–45, Nanzen-ji Temple, Kyoto, photograph courtesy of Machiro Tanaka/Pacific Press Service; p. 52, Biblioteca Real, El Escorial, Madrid, photograph courtesy of Giraudon/Art Resource; p. 57, courtesy of the Freer Gallery of Art, Smithsonian Institution, Washington, DC; p. 59, photograph courtesy of Werner Forman; p. 61, photograph courtesy of AKG London; p. 71, photograph courtesy of John Edwards/ Zoological Society of London; p. 77, Sri Partap Singh Museum, Srinagar, photograph courtesy of AKG London/Jean-Louis Nou; p. 84, Victoria & Albert Museum, London, photograph courtesy of Bridgeman Art Library/SuperStock; p. 101, photograph courtesy of National Zoological Park, Smithsonian Institution/Jessie Cohen

A CIP catalogue record for this book is available from the British Library

ISBN 1 86046 677 X

Printed in the United States of America
Designed by Jonathan D. Lippincott
Map designed by Jeffrey L. Ward

This book is respectfully dedicated to the tiger biologists cited in this book who recognize that if their work is to have lasting significance, it can no longer confine itself to field research but must also include advocacy and public education and other elements of conservation that might slow the diminishment, not only of Panthera tigris, *but of biodiversity and all life on earth.*

In particular, I am very grateful to those whose advice, hospitality, and help has been invaluable in my own tiger research, including Maurice Hornocker, Howard Quigley, Dale Miquelle, Evgeny Smirnov, Anatoli Astafiev, Dimitri Pikunov (Russian Far East); Kim Soo-il (Korea); Alexander Matthiessen (Indonesia); Belinda Wright, Fateh Singh Rahore, Valmik Thapar, George Schaller, Ullas Karanth, Bittu Sahgal, Ramachaudra Gupta (India); Alan Rabinowitz (Southeast Asia); John Seidensticker (Indonesia, Nepal); Ginette Hemley of the World Wildlife Fund and Kristin Nowell, a consultant to WWF and TRAFFIC (tiger medicine trade). It was Dr. Hornocker who first welcomed me to the Siberian Tiger Project in the Russian Far East and Drs. Quigley and Miquelle who were my kind hosts and mentors on a second visit. Dr. Seidensticker, curator of mammals at the Smithsonian National Zoological Park and an authority on the tigers of Indonesia and the Indian subcontinent, has endorsed and guided my research throughout with unfailing exactitude and generosity.

To hunt the tiger, you must first hunt the tiger in yourself, and to do that you first make certain that the tiger is not hunting you.

—Mochtar Lubis, *Tiger! Tiger!*

All genuine knowledge originates in direct experience.

—Mao Tse-tung

Future generations would be truly saddened that this century had so little foresight, so little compassion, such lack of generosity of spirit for the future that it would eliminate one of the most dramatic and beautiful animals this world has ever seen.   —George Schaller

Everyone is connected. Only the tiger is not connected.

—Vladimir Shetinin, commander (retired) of Operation Amba

When you see a tiger, it is always like a dream.

—Ullas Karanth

INTRODUCTION

Our Siberian Tiger Project began in 1989 on the other side of the world in central Idaho's Frank Church River of No Return Wilderness. My colleague at the Hornocker Wildlife Research Institute, Howard Quigley, was helping to entertain a visiting delegation from the Soviet Academy of Sciences. At a campfire gathering at a remote field station where Howard and I had conducted mountain lion research, the subject of Siberian tigers came up. The lead scientist in the Soviet group, Dr. Yuri Puzachenko, vice chairman of the powerful academy, issued an invitation for us to visit Moscow and the Far East to explore the possibility of an intensive research effort on the Siberian tiger. Dr. Puzachenko, a jovial, outgoing man and one of the most respected scientists in Russia, assured us he would "clear the way" for us in the then-Communist bureaucracy.

So it happened that, in January 1990, Howard and I stepped from an Aeroflot jet into the frigid Vladivostok air. Awaiting us was a stern-looking lineup of Russian scientists. We had been warned of scientific territorialism in "the East," and no strangers to this phenomenon in U.S. academic circles, we wondered what lay ahead.

Dr. Dimitri Pikunov was the first to step forward. Powerfully built, with steely blue eyes set in a weathered face, he was the Russian tiger specialist best known to us, because of his writings. He would also prove to be one of our strongest allies and best friends. Also on hand were tiger experts Evgeny Smirnov, Igor Nikolaev, Victor Yudin, Victor Korkishko, and Anatoli Astafiev, manager of the Sikhote-Alin State Biosphere Reserve. After the initial greetings, we were escorted to a brand-new Nissan and whisked off to a charming little hotel on the outskirts of the city, a favorite haunt of Communist brass visiting from Moscow.

In this quiet, countrylike atmosphere, we talked tigers with our hosts for two days and nights. We found them surprisingly knowledgeable about our work despite their isolation from most of the rest of the scientific world. Some were now in administrative positions, but all were true field naturalists possessing a wealth of information gained by years of experience in the field, even though their research on tigers had been limited to observations and snow tracking. They were eager to work with Howard and me to apply modern technology to their studies.

Following our meetings in Vladivostok, we were taken on a tour of known tiger range throughout the Russian Far East. We were especially eager to visit the Sikhote-Alin Reserve, a wildlife reserve the size of Yosemite Park some 300 miles northeast of Vladivostok on the coast of the Sea of Japan; we'd been told Sikhote-Alin was the best place to study tigers. Our flight took us across mountains not unlike our Pacific Coast range and up a relatively pristine coastline to Terney, a fishing village and headquarters for the reserve.

For the next several days we explored Sikhote-Alin. Evgeny Smirnov, the reserve's lead tiger biologist, took us straight to areas of tiger activity. He showed us tracks—made only the night before—within a quarter mile of our cabin. He took us to a ridge-top crossing where a huge male had lain in the deep snow, presumably on the lookout for the wild boar or red deer numerous in that area. We saw tracks of a mother and two cubs within sight of the outskirts of Terney. Truly, Howard and I agreed, we were in tiger country.

And yet tiger numbers had been extremely low when Sikhote-Alin was established—some estimate only about fifty individuals. Once plentiful throughout Siberia, from Lake Baikal east to the coast and south into China and Korea, the Siberian tiger (also called the Amur tiger) had been hunted relentlessly for its skin and body parts—important in Asian folk medicine—and had disappeared from most of its former range. Ironically, it began a recovery under Communist rule, when closed borders limited legitimate trade such as lumbering and illegitimate activities like poaching. By 1985 there were an estimated 450 tigers in the Sikhote-Alin—a remarkable comeback, we thought, although the Russian scientists cautioned that 450 tigers was really not so many. (Little did we suspect that scarcely two years later, with the dissolution of the Soviet Union and the opening of its borders, tigers would again be under siege.)

We left Sikhote-Alin Reserve greatly encouraged by what we had seen and experienced. The tigers were certainly there, the officials and scientists welcomed us and urged the study, the people were warm and friendly. And the landscape, little known to the Western world, was breathtaking. As the big old Aeroflot helicopter lifted off the snowy field at Terney, Howard and I knew we would be back.

We spent the next several days flying to outposts and villages in the Bikin River drainage, the last stronghold of the Udege, the native people who still revere the tiger. When an elderly Udege woman, a longtime friend of Dr. Pikunov, asked why we Americans were there, he replied that we wanted to help save the tiger. She replied that only the Udege were really concerned about the tiger's well-being. Besides, she said good-naturedly, "Americans are like flies—they are everywhere."

On the long flight back to Moscow—passing through seven time zones—Howard and I mapped our strategy. We knew what awaited us in Moscow—excruciating sessions with a hard-nosed Russian negotiator, literally locked in a hotel room. Our predictions were painfully accurate. Reeling from fatigue and conceding practically every point of contention, some eighteen hours later we emerged with a joint Russian-American agreement for the study of the Siberian tiger. We took some solace in the knowledge that such an agreement was essential to our effort to raise the necessary research funding.

Nevertheless, at first no one would consider committing long-term, significant funding for work in Communist Russia. Finally, the National Geographic Society awarded us a generous grant. Their support convinced others to help, notably the National Fish and Wildlife Foundation and the National Wildlife Federation. So, on January 1, 1992, almost two years after our initial visit (and after an additional fact-finding trip), Howard and Kathy Quigley, Dale Miquelle, and I arrived in Far Eastern Russia to begin the actual field research. Kathy, Howard's wife, is project veterinarian, highly trained in carnivore tranquillization. Dale had spent a year studying tigers in Nepal and had recently completed his doctorate studying moose in Denali Park in Alaska.

Our research approach was straightforward—study the tiger and its habitat and establish a solid foundation of knowledge. This would include all information about the tiger's biology and ecology, its life needs and its behavior. We would also study the animals that tigers prey upon and the total environment in which they lived. With this knowledge, we would be in a strong position to make recommendations to government authorities—and to local residents—on what measures must be taken to save the tiger.

In studying a secretive species like tigers, direct observation is impossible. Instead, we observe them indirectly by utilizing radio-telemetry. Each tiger is captured with a cable snare, and a collar carrying a small transmitter is placed on its neck. The transmitter sends an identifying signal, allowing us to monitor tigers from season to season and from year to year, gaining information on individuals and on the population at large.

In February 1992, Howard, Kathy, and Dale, along with Igor Nikolaev and Evgeny Smirnov, captured and collared a Siberian tiger. In June 1992 we made our second capture—a big, mature tigress we named Lena. Since then we have placed radio collars on twenty more tigers. From monitoring these tigers—some for seven years now—we know how much space they require, what they eat, how often they breed, what becomes of the young, how they react to human activities, and what makes for good tiger habitat. We now have the information that can save the Siberian tiger from extinction.

Working with our Russian colleagues, we submitted a tiger habitat protection plan to the Russian Ministry of the Environment in Moscow. They have adopted this plan as part of the government's official plan for tiger conservation. We have worked with Dr. Astafiev at Sikhote-Alin to implement his plan to expand the reserve to incorporate critical tiger habitat—an expansion that could be compared to enlarging Yellowstone by 20 percent to provide for grizzly bears or bison. We secured the funding in the United States to accomplish this from the Exxon Corporation, through the Save the Tiger Fund.

It is fact, however, that any conservation program, anywhere in the world, requires attention to more than just biology. A successful conservation program must consider economics, politics, and the human culture. From the beginning, we have attempted to address all these factors. But before we could be effective, we had to gain credibility. We did so through hard work and a spirit of cooperation. We hired the three top Russian tiger specialists; we hired and trained young Russian technicians and aides; we provided for Russian student participation, working with their advisors at the University of Moscow. We created a truly cooperative effort at the local and regional levels. We not only worked alongside our Russian colleagues on a daily basis, we bought property, when it became possible to do so, and moved into neighborhoods in the village of Terney. In other words, we became part of the community.

Now when we urge sustained-yield forestry practices, for example, we do so in a unified, Russian-American voice. And when we discuss alternatives to such traditional extractive industries as mining and logging, we speak with the support of our Russian colleagues. In the past, commerce in sustainable forest products such as berries, nuts, mushrooms, ginseng, and wild honey flourished in many communities. We are working with community leaders to revive many of these economically viable cottage industries. Such practices can enhance a forest ecosystem for tigers and their prey while providing for the people.

For it is essential that local and regional people be convinced it is in their best interest to conserve rather than to kill tigers. And in order for that to happen, there must be a viable economy in place that sustains rather than destroys the forest. If we can bring about favorable economic development—favorable to the forest and to tigers— politics and politicians will be on our side.

Cultural factors can be powerful forces in conservation, sometimes more powerful than economic or political concerns. There are numerous examples from old cultures—sacred cows in India, cranes in Japan, tigers to the Udege. More recently, in North America, for example, birds of prey, considered vermin in rural areas since European settlement, are now protected and have become symbols of conservation success. Even sharks are shedding their evil image. Big carnivores like wolves and mountain lions are held inviolate and are admired by millions. Grizzly bears, once limited to restricted areas in national parks, are being considered for reintroduction into their traditional range.

In the Russian Far East, we are making an effort to promote tigers as such symbols, so that one day it will be culturally unacceptable to kill them anywhere, for any reason. This step requires education at all levels, and not only where tigers live but internationally as well.

I first met Peter Matthiessen in Terney in June 1992. Long an admirer of his writing and his conservation ethic, I had invited him to visit the Siberian Tiger Project early on. Howard and I felt that he, with his incredible insight and sensitivity to both environmental and cultural issues, could perhaps better than anyone else focus international attention on the plight of the Siberian tiger.

He readily agreed to come and, as luck would have it, arrived almost in time to see a tiger—our capture of Lena had occurred two days before. But in the ensuing time together, we found common ground on a great many fronts and became fast friends.

Three years later, Peter visited Sikhote-Alin again. Exploring the region with Howard Quigley, Dale Miquelle, and our Russian colleagues, he gained further insight into the problems facing tiger conservation and the role local cultures must play in it and also observed his first "tiger in the snow."

No one can articulate these elements as well as Peter. No one can place human cultures in their environment—as integral part and parcel of their natural environment—as well as Peter. My colleagues and I, both American and Russian, are privileged that he is contributing so much to our efforts to save the great "Amba," the "Protector of the Forest," the most magnificent of all the great cats. This book is testimony to his commitment.

ABOUT THE PHOTOGRAPHS

On our first visit to the Russian Far East in January 1990, Howard Quigley and I met Professor Victor Yudin of the Soviet Academy of Sciences in Vladivostok, a career-long student of animal behavior, who spoke of the orphaned tiger cubs he had rescued earlier that winter. Two tigresses had been shot after threatening villagers in separate occurrences in a remote region, leaving four orphaned cubs. Two of the malnourished cubs had died, but he had nursed a male and a female back to health. He told us his plans for a facility where he could conduct behavioral studies of the pair and perhaps breed them when they became sexually mature.

Professor Yudin (see photo p. 24) constructed his facility 186.3 kilometers north of Vladivostok, near the remote village of Gayvoron. Its five acres enclosed the oak forest and riparian vegetation native to the tiger's range; the tigers were released into a forest type no different from that inhabited by their wild cousins. Over the years we cooperated with Yudin in a number of experiments designed to give us insights into the inherent and learned behavior of tigers. Some of the results helped us to evaluate and understand the behavior of tigers living in the wild.

Most of the photographs appearing in this book were taken in different seasons over a period of years at Yudin's facility. Despite much effort, we have been able to obtain only a few photos of wild Siberians (see, for example, p. 132), which, unlike the tigers of India and Nepal, have never become habituated to people but have remained truly wild even in the reserves. Only a few photographs of wild Siberians are known to exist, and most of those are of dead tigers.

The photographs here, while taken at Professor Yudin's facility, accurately depict this splendid animal in its native Siberian habitat, doing what wild tigers do each day. If these photographs stir the conservation embers in readers' souls and help to save the great Siberian, then our efforts will have been well rewarded.

—Maurice Hornocker

TIGERS IN THE SNOW

The beautiful wild region known as the Russian Far East curves south along the Sea of Japan like a great claw of Siberia, from the vast delta of the Amur River to the North Korean border, and its coast range—the Sikhote-Alin—extending southward some 600 miles between the Ussuri River and the sea is the last redoubt of *Panthera tigris altaica*, the Siberian or Manchurian tiger, which ranged formerly throughout northeastern China (or Manchuria) and the Korean peninsula, and west as far as Mongolia and Lake Baikal. In the past century, its range has been reduced almost entirely to the Amur-Ussuri watershed, and today the most appropriate name for the largest of the world's great cats is the Amur tiger.

The Sikhote-Alin, at latitude 40 to 50.5 degrees, is a range of

mountains rarely more than 6,000 feet high. Its forest is temperate pine-and-hardwood *taiga* with fir and spruce at higher altitudes, subsiding as it descends in the north into boreal conifers of spruce-muskeg tundra (the original taiga, or "land of little sticks," refers to those stunted spruce; today the term is used more often as a rough equivalent of "wilderness"). Here the brown bear, lynx, wolf, and sable of the north cross tracks with the black bear, tiger, and leopard of the broad-leafed forests farther south, in an astonishing mammalian fauna—unlike any other left on earth.

Ussuria or Ussuri Land was all but unknown to the West until early in the twentieth century, when it was explored by Vladimir K. Arseniev, a young army lieutenant, geographer, and naturalist who made three expeditions there between 1902 and 1908 in order to map the wild Primorski Krai, or Maritime Province. Arseniev was subsequently described as "the great explorer of Eastern Siberia" by the

Peter Matthiessen

Arctic explorer Fridtjof Nansen, who expressed astonishment that this region of the Asian land mass had remained less known than the wildest Indian countries of North America.

Traveling on horseback and on foot, Arseniev was guided by a man named Dersu, an indigenous hunter-trapper of the Tungus-Manchu tribes (Altaic Tatar peoples related to the Tibetans and Mongolians and also to those ancient hunters who traveled east across the Chukchi Peninsula and Beringia to North America). As a young man, Dersu had survived a terrible mauling by a tiger; he was exhausted and near death from loss of blood when his wife found him in the taiga after days of tracking.

Like all aboriginal hunters, Dersu feared the tiger's immense strength and ferocity but also revered it as the very breath and spirit of the taiga. These Tungus peoples considered it a near-deity and sometimes addressed it as "Grandfather" or "Old Man." The indigenous Udege and Nanai tribes referred to it as "Amba" or "tiger" (it was only the white strangers—the Russians—who translated that word as "devil"). To the Manchurians, the tiger was Hu Lin, the king, since the head and nape stripes on certain mythic individuals resembled the character Wan-da—the great sovereign or prince. "On a tree nearby fluttered a red flag," Arseniev wrote, "with the inscription: *San men dshen vei Si-zhi-tsi-go vei da suay Tsin tsan da tsin chezhen shan-lin,*' which means 'To the True Spirit of the Mountains: in antiquity in the dynasty of Tsi he was commander-in-chief for the dynasty Da Tsin, but now he guards the forests and mountains.' "

Because the tiger protected the precious ginseng root from the Manchurians, Dersu would never shoot at Amba, and he entreated Arseniev not to shoot him, either. (Indigenous peoples throughout

southern Asia avoided killing tigers, all except man-eaters, and even then might hold a ceremony of regret in which it was explained to other tigers how their kinsman had erred and must now forfeit its life.) Arseniev and Dersu, exploring Ussuri Land in every season, had many encounters with Amba, to whom they lost their dog, and one day the lieutenant expressed regret that he had never actually laid eyes on this secretive presence. Dersu cried out, "Oh no! Bad see him! Men [who] never see Amba . . . happy, lucky men . . . Me see Amba much. One time shot, miss. Now me very much fear. For me now one day will be bad, bad luck." (In keeping with the conventions of the era, Dersu's speech was rendered in the same pidgin English spoken to white sahibs by Indian scouts, African bearers, and other trusty native guides in memoirs from all around the colonial world.) Amba pervades Arseniev's journals, an imminent menace that the doughty Russian begins to dread. "We stood there silently a few minutes in the hope that some sound would betray the presence of the tiger, but there was the silence of the grave. In that silence I felt mystery, and fear."

In Arseniev's time, the tiger was already under heavy pressure from foreign hunters. Both Russians and Manchurian Chinese claimed these remote hunting grounds, which were rich in the precious ginseng root and the lustrous fur of the large arboreal weasel called the sable; these invading strangers, and the Koreans, too, ignored the rights of the indigenous peoples, who were mainly discounted as *tazi* by the Russians (from the Chinese *da-tsi*, or "foreigners"—that is, "others") despite their long prior habitation— at least 6,000 years, according to the carbon dating of petroglyphs found along the upper Amur, which include representations of the great northern tiger that in other days was found there, too.

Tiger and elk, Iron Age leather saddle, Siberia

• • •

The primary habitat of the Amur tiger is the taiga or temperate woodland from sea level to 3,000 feet, in a climate where winter temperatures may fall as low as $-40°F$, with snow twelve to twenty inches deep for four months of the year. Prey animals in these mixed hardwood forests included the large red deer (or wapiti or elk), the spotted or sika deer, the small roe deer, the Asian goral (a brown, goatlike creature of the Eurasian family called goat-antelopes), and the wild pig or "wild boar," which in Arseniev's day apparently attained a weight of over 600 pounds. For all of these prey animals, the tiger competed with the leopard in the south and the wolf in the north and also with brown and black bears, which are primarily vegetarian but also opportunists; the brown bear will often dispute a tiger's kill. (In the many accounts of bear-tiger confrontations, both animals are alleged to have been the victors; however, it is commonly agreed that the bear, prefers to contest the much smaller female tiger, lest it become an item of tiger diet.) Other inhabitants of the Sikhote-Alin and the Ussuri Valley noted by Arseniev were moose and musk deer, lynx, sable, badger, fox, hare, polecat, otter, and a squat canid animal with a dark "mask" called the raccoon dog, in addition to various squirrels and sundry chipmunks, gophers, water rats, moles, voles, and shrews. (The one large animal he does not mention is the leopard, though it must have been widespread in southern Ussuri Land.)

As early as their second expedition, in 1906, Dersu was saying, "All round soon all game end. Me think ten years, no more wapiti, no more sable, no more squirrel, all gone." And Arseniev comments, "It was impossible to disagree with him. In their own country, the Chinese have long since exterminated the game, almost every living thing. All that is

left to them are crows, dogs, and rats . . . The Primorski-Amur country, so rich in forest and wildlife, awaits the same fate." Even now, he reports, the Chinese were "ransacking" the land, hunting the sable, wapiti, and musk deer (for its precious musk gland); gathering ginseng, roots, and oils; cultivating the wild poppy for opium; collecting pearls, seaweeds, crabs and lobsters, and *trepang* (sea slugs) along the coast; even scraping the tasteless *Parmelia* lichen ("stone's skin") off the rocks. "On every side one sees nothing but robbery and exploitation. In the not-distant future this land of Ussuria . . . will be turned into a desert."

In the decade after Dersu's grim prediction, the tiger was heavily hunted as a sport by naval and army officers at the great eastern military base of Vladivostok, and in the chaotic early

Elk (or red deer)

years of the Russian Revolution, both White and Red soldiery, living off the forest and shooting everything in sight, drove the animal to near-extinction. In the 1920s, when the Soviet Socialist Republics were established, the surviving tigers were hammered hard by Communist Party nimrods, who might bag eight or ten on a single outing, and from the 1930s until the 1950s, when it was realized that the animals were disappearing, there was urgent collection of young cubs for the world's zoos, a practice that often involved shooting the mother.

By 1935, when the Manchurian Chinese were driven back across the Amur and the Ussuri, the tiger had already withdrawn from its northern and western range, and the few that remained in the East Manchurian Mountains near Ussuria's borders with China and Korea were being cut off from the main population in Ussuri Land by new roads and railroads that served agricultural settlement of the Ussuri Valley. Meanwhile, its former habitats in Manchuria were ruthlessly deforested and settled by Han Chinese, brought in to displace the ethnic Manchurians, much as the Han are displacing the Tibetans of today. (In China, the Amur is called Heilongjiang, which means "Black Dragon River," and Manchuria has become "the Northeastern Provinces" of Jilin and Heilongjiang.) Within a few years, the last viable population of *P. t. altaica* was confined to Ussuri Land in Dersu's magnificent country of pine and hardwood taiga, mountains, and blue sea.

In 1936, when the Sikhote-Alin Reserve was established on the north Primorski coast, perhaps fifty scattered animals remained; four years later, tiger authority K. G. Kaplanov would estimate that but twenty were left in all of the Maritime Province. However, during World War II, with Russian hunters off in Europe shooting at other members of their own species, *P. t. altaica* made a small recovery. In 1947, shooting tigers was officially prohibited in Russia, and in 1962, the last *altaica* in Heilongjiang, across the Ussuri River, received protection. Within the decade, special permits were required for collecting cubs, and in the mid-1980s, with continuing state protection (the wildlife reserves or *zapovedniki* had remained closed to the public), researcher Dimitri Pikunov of the Russian Academy of Science's Far Eastern branch would estimate a population of 250 Amur tigers—a significant recovery that justified the hope of reestablishing a viable wild population.

Then, in 1989, in the chaos attending the quickening collapse of the Soviet Union, law and order broke down almost entirely. Siberia's natural resources, from timber to wildlife, were sold and traded like hot chestnuts in the streets, whether or not the seller was the lawful owner, and unpaid zapovedniki officials and forest rangers in the penniless wildlife departments were increasingly susceptible to bribes. Most of the tigers lived and were killed outside the zapovedniki, but inside, too, uncontrolled logging and mining, splitting the forests with rough roads, was destroying good habitat for the tiger and its prey and providing easy access for the hunters. Modern firearms, formerly prohibited and scarce, were now available, and so were new vehicles equipped with four-wheel drive. The great forests of the Sikhote-Alin were under siege by Korean, Japanese, and American corporations seeking a foothold in this region, and a surging Pacific Rim economy ever more inflated by globalization created an increased demand for traditional tiger medicines throughout East Asia, as Siberia's once-rigid borders were laid wide to smuggling for this wildly profitable market. By January 1992, when a Russian-American tiger research project was formally established in the Sikhote-Alin Reserve, more than a third of the remaining Amur tigers had already

Peter Matthiessen

been destroyed, and *P. t. altaica* was once again in serious danger of extinction.

Like most wide-eyed children in the West, I knew from my awed scrutiny of the great roaring cats of zoo and circus almost all that was worth knowing about the tiger's sinister black knife stripes, scary fangs, and flashing claws. I was also well steeped in a thrilling children's book called *The Story of Little Black Sambo*, whimsically written and colorfully illustrated by an English gentlewoman, resident in India for thirty years, who, as a colonial of the British Raj, never bothered her head about useless distinctions between one group of dark-skinned "natives" and another. It is true that certain aboriginal tribes of the Indian subcontinent are very dark and even "black," but they lack the pronounced African features that Helen Bannerman bestowed on her young hero and his family—a confusion that helped disseminate the notion, widespread in the West, that tigers dwell in Africa with lions. (While the lion was formerly widespread in southern Eurasia as well as Africa and still persists in the Gir Forest of western India, no trace of tiger has ever been found outside Asia.) In these more enlightened times, Bannerman's little book has understandably displeased the politically correct among readers of all colors, who have seen to it that its title, text, and illustrations have been changed.

In the original story, the greedy tigers, chasing one another around a tree in pursuit of the little boy's bright clothes, reduce themselves to golden puddles of ghee butter—and quite fitting, too, since in all traditional Asian cultures, a tiger is perceived as protean, ever-changing, a fearsome animal yet at times beneficent, and often associated with the sacred. ("The Tiger Is God," read the banner of Tipu Sultan, an Indian moghul of the eighteenth century.) In many cultures, the tiger, like the crane, is regarded as an intermediary between heaven and earth, traveling great distances on its healing missions; it is also capable of creating rain and shepherding lost children. But in Hindu mythologies, unlike most of the others, the tiger is perceived more often as a source of evil; sometimes the destroyer Shiva is portrayed with a fierce tiger visage or wearing a tiger's skin, and both Shiva and his consort, Parvati, may be depicted riding on a tiger. In Buddhist symbology, it is one of "the Three Senseless Creatures," manifesting anger (as the monkey manifests greed and the deer folly). It is probably the subject of more varied myths and endowed with more fanciful attributes than any other creature known to man.

This negative view of the great tiger pervades Rudyard Kipling's *The Jungle Book*, with its wonderful descriptions of the man-eater Shere Khan ("The moonlight was blocked out of the mouth of the cave, for Shere Khan's great square head and shoulders were thrust into the entrance . . . Am I to stand nosing into your dog den for my fair dues? It is I, Shere Khan, who speak!"). Yet the hunter Jim Corbett, in his laconic accounts of hunting dangerous tiger and leopard in *The Man-eaters of Kumaon*, refers to the tiger as "a large-hearted gentleman of bottomless courage."

Not until the 1960s would I come across *Dersu the Trapper*, Arseniev's obscure masterpiece, long out of print—the first account I had ever read of the so-called Siberian tiger and my first realization that the Indian or Royal Bengal tiger of Kipling and Corbett was only one geographic population of a species that formerly occurred in

an astonishing variety of Asian habitats, from the sub-Arctic to the equatorial tropics. Reading Arseniev's accounts, I envisioned a huge primordial tiger, shaggy and frost-tipped, shambling along the seacoast in the snow; I was filled with yearning to travel to Ussuri Land. A few years later, I wrote a film treatment based on the Siberian tiger—in the fevered parlance of the film's producer, the "rarest, largest, and most secretive flesh-eater prowling this earth today." At that time, most of the Soviet Union had been closed to foreigners for decades, but after eight years of negotiations with the authorities in Moscow, the film company had finally received permission to travel to Ussuri Land for its locations. The screen treatment had been approved when the permit was withdrawn abruptly and forever, presumably because the Ussuri country lay too close to Vladivostok, with its closed port and Cold War military installations. By 1990, when I first visited Siberia on an expedition to Lake Baikal, the late great film director Akira Kurosawa had already made his beautiful *Dersu Uzala.*

The Siberian Tiger Project, a joint effort of Russian tiger authorities and American wildlife biologists, was one of the first "foreign" operations permitted into the Russian Far East after 1989—in effect, a research program designed to study the ecology and habitat requirements of *P. t. altaica* as the basis for a comprehensive plan to try to save it. In addition, the project would cooperate with local government in public education about tigers, encourage general conservation, and assist the Sikhote-Alin zapovednik staff in acquiring more tiger habitat by seeking to enlarge its present boundaries. It was also committed to raising funds for the first organized anti-poaching patrols in the reserve.

The American co-directors of the project, Maurice Hornocker

and Howard Quigley of the Hornocker Wildlife Research Institute (affiliated with the University of Idaho), had been pioneers in the use of radio telemetry in field studies of the mountain lion and jaguar, respectively. In the early 1970s, Dr. Hornocker had been invited by Russian scientists to come to the Amur region and teach them telemetry techniques, a plan approved by the Soviet government only to be disallowed by the Nixon administration. Twenty years would pass before he was welcomed to what was now the Sikhote-Alin State Biosphere Reserve, the largest wildlife reserve in the Far East, with 1,350 square miles of forested mountains, silver torrents, and unbroken coast. The tiger project would be based in the reserve headquarters at Terney, a fishing and logging port 350 miles northeast of Vladivostok that was all but surrounded by the forest. By January 1, 1992, the Siberian Tiger Project was under way.

Howard Quigley (right) and forest guard Victor Voronin inspect tracks of female tiger and cubs

Peter Matthiessen

In the first month, the researchers set the heavy box traps that the Russians thought might work, but pugmarks showed that from the start, the tigers were wary of the large boxes and went out of their way to avoid them. After five weeks or so, the huge crates were replaced by foot snares, used successfully in the United States on bear and cougar. Buried unbaited in likely places such as game trails, these snares were activated by a spring that draws a padded noose tight just above the claws, though not so tight that it breaks the skin or impedes circulation.

One day in early February, a local hunter, Volodya Velichko, notified the researchers that a fresh tiger kill could be found only two miles north of Terney, across the river delta in the coastal dunes. For the next two nights, in the bitter cold, Howard Quigley and a young biologist named Dale Miquelle set snares on the dead elk after midnight, checking them at daylight to ensure that a tiger would not be held captive longer than necessary. When no tiger was snared, they suspended trapping. When they returned four or five days later, they found a new kill about 300 yards away which the tiger had dragged down the slope, away from the older carcass. A snare was set near the fresh kill, and when they returned next morning with Velichko and Kathy Quigley, the project veterinarian, they found Study Animal #1, a fine young tigress. Once she was sedated by a tranquillizer dart fired from a shotgun, the team took the tigress's weight and measurements and a blood specimen, then fitted her with a radio collar, trying to work quickly in spite of the 6°F temperature that coagulated tiger blood and froze their pens as well as hands. Later the blood sample would be analyzed to determine its genetic composition and to locate any evidence of inbreeding in the tiger population. The team was finished in an hour, and the tigress was up and gone. On February 16, 1992, the first marked Amur tiger (165 pounds, twelve to fourteen months old) had been captured and returned to the wild, wearing the thick radio collar that would allow the scientists to monitor her activities and whereabouts. Next day she was seen a mile from the capture site, crouched on a goral kill made by her mother.

That first young tigress, nicknamed Olga, was still the lone marked animal when, in late June 1992, I secured a place on a flight from Khabarovsk to the mining town at Kavalierova, in the south Sikhote-Alin. From there Russian associates of Dr. Hornocker provided a ride north on the rough, lonely road that follows the coast range 150 miles to Terney. Near Rudnaya Pristan ("Raw Materials Port"), where the minerals and timber of Primorski Krai join the great flow of Siberia's natural resources overseas, we stayed the night at the Institute of Geography, which, like most government facilities in the new Russia, was sadly empty and decrepit for want of funding. I arrived at Terney at midmorning next day—two days too late, as it turned out, to witness the capture and release of Tiger #2, a tigress whom the researchers had christened Lena.

In *Dersu the Trapper*, Arseniev mentions the "famous Bay of Terney," discovered by "the famous La Pérouse" on July 23, 1767. "The view up the valley from the sea is fine. The lofty hills with their sharp and capricious peaks look magnificent . . . and produced . . . an impression of wild beauty . . . The valley is covered with a fine mixed forest, with many fine cedars [the valuable Korean pine] . . . The all-devouring hand of the timber merchant had not yet touched this virgin forest."

Peter Matthiessen

Maurice Hornocker and Dale Miquelle with collared tiger

Terney is a small logging and fishing community and county center where many people find work in the provincial bureaucracies.
With its small wood cottages, zinc green and faded blue, its vegetable
gardens and picket fences, outhouses, guard dogs, and trim woodpiles,
and its birch-shaded mud lanes twisting uphill and inland toward the
mountains, Old Terney appeared to have changed little since Arseniev's visit early in the century, although the Manchurian Chinese
were long since gone.

Maurice Hornocker, a rangy, well-weathered wildlife biologist in
his mid-fifties whom I first encountered on the village street, is probably the world's foremost authority on the great cats. He introduced
me to wildlife biologist Dale Miquelle and also to two Russian scientists, Igor Nikolaev and Evgeny Smirnov, who have both had exten-

sive field experience with *P. t. altaica*. Smirnov calls this zapovednik "the Predator Reserve," since tiger and lynx and wolf and brown and black bear are all present, with lesser carnivores of the fierce weasel tribe—sable and mink, wolverine and badger, weasel and the yellow-throated marten—working the edges. (The wild dog known as the *dhole* is now extinct in Russia, although it occurred in southern Ussuria until the 1970s; the peculiar canid called the raccoon dog remains quite common.) When Smirnov first came here from Moscow as a mouse biologist in 1963, the tiger had been extirpated from the reserve for nearly a decade. Within three years, a few wanderers appeared, then one female produced cubs. When a small population became established, Smirnov's interest switched from mice to tigers, and his data and observations from thirty-odd years in the Sikhote-Alin represent the longest continuous study ever undertaken of this animal.

Evgeny Smirnov

Smirnov's colleague Igor Nikolaev, of the Academy of Sciences in Vladivostok, is also a consultant on the Siberian Tiger Project. Nikolaev worked for many years with the noted tiger biologist A. G. Yudakov, his co-author in *The Ecology of the Amur Tiger*. (A few years ago, pinned by a felled tree while alone in the forest, Dr. Yudakov dug himself out by chipping frozen dirt from beneath his shattered leg, then crawled and dragged himself toward a settlement. Although still alive when found, he died in hospital a few weeks later.) Nikolaev is rather quiet and speaks shyly, but in the awed opinion of Dale

Miquelle, "Igor knows more about the Amur tiger in the wild than any man alive." In the absence of funds for radio telemetry equipment, tiger research in Russia had been largely based on tracking animals on foot in winter. While a good deal of basic information on tiger numbers and travel routes, predation, scent-making, and other behavior had been obtained, data could be gathered only when snow covered the ground. What radio telemetry made possible was the first year-round study of Amur tiger behavior ever undertaken, and also the first "longitudinal studies" following known individuals through the four seasons.

The researchers were en route to the airstrip, and I went along. In an old AN-2 biplane with a 1,000-HP radial engine, we climbed laboriously into the air and headed north over the low coast range, whose highest peak is 6,575 feet.

Ussuria and Heilongjiang, like northern Japan, are composed of what biogeographers know as "Manchu-Japanese mixed forest," and slightly more than 70 percent of both Primorski Krai and southern Khabarovski Krai, which together comprise about 95 percent of *altaica*'s remaining range, have remained forested. From the air, the unbroken wilderness, rising toward the western ridges and descending again into the Ussuri Valley, seemed utterly unspoiled. Dark forests of Korean pine ascend these mountains, with fir and spruce above 2,500 feet; at lower elevations near the coast, a mixed pine and hardwood taiga is dominated by oak and birch.

Using earphones and the radio, the researchers attempted to find their two tigers. Soon Olga's signal was located north of Terney, and the plane crisscrossed steep wooded slopes and sunny ledges, gold-leafed oak woods with dark islets of pine where the mountains descended to sheer precipice, white surf, and the dark stone blue of the Sea of Japan. The ungulate animals preyed upon by tigers prefer hillside and stream valley habitats near the sea in which hardwoods, pine, and secondary growth provide food and cover. Cone nuts from the Korean pine and acorns from the Mongolian oak are critical mast for the wild pigs and the deer species as well as for other forest creatures, from bears to squirrels. Though Olga remained hidden under the canopy, the signals from her transmitter revealed that she was moving and presumably in good health. (The transmitters broadcast one signal when the tiger is at rest and another when it is active, with a different frequency for each study animal.)

Roaring and shuddering, the biplane swung up and away, recrossing the beautiful Serebryanka River to the region of Lena's capture site in the south of the reserve. Unlike Olga, this tigress was not moving, which is normal in the middle of the day. However, her signal was still coming from a wooded drainage less than a mile from her capture site. Full recovery from the shock of capture may take two to three days, but the biologists were quietly concerned that Lena had not recovered faster and wandered farther.

Next day, in hopes of discovering what ailed her, we trekked into the forest, following the Khanov Creek upstream for several miles through hardwood taiga of oak and birch, basswood and maple, poplar, ash, and elm, with scattered pines. In the fresh airy greenwood of late June, wherever sunlight sifted through the canopy, were violets and buttercups, wild roses and strawberries, iris, lady's slipper, phlox, wild grape—a flora of the Northern Hemisphere that seemed strangely out of place in a haunt of tigers. But on a dim trail all but closed over by ferns were big raw pugmarks, then a fresh scrape. Perhaps these had been made by Lena, perhaps not.

Attacks on man by the great Amur tiger were recorded as early as 1870, in the accounts of the explorer Nikolai Prezhewalski, discoverer of the huge shallow Lake Khanka on the Ussuria-Manchuria border and also of the wild horse of the steppes that bears his name; there are also accounts of "Manchurian tigers" that in 1923 plagued the construction of the Trans-Baikal railway until "they became a positive pest, killing and carrying off workmen, till a regiment of Cossacks had to be sent in to cope with the situation." Yet a species account of 1961 by tiger authority V. K. Abramov would assert that this tiger never attacked men: "During all the years since the Revolution not a single case of a man-eater has been reported." Perhaps the contradiction is explained by the fact that in the period cited by Abramov, the Amur tiger was very near extinction.

At any rate, awareness that a tiger is close by lends a certain edge to walking in the taiga. Scrapes were numerous among the ferns of the forest floor, and a fine big print in the dried mud sprang at the eye. ("The perfectly distinct and fresh impressions of an immense cat's paw, standing out sharply printed in the muddy track," as Arseniev describes it. The water had not yet found its way into this quite-fresh pugmark.) High up on a tree trunk, deep scratches marked the place where a tiger on hind legs had sharpened its two-inch claws by raking them downward with the powerful foreshoulders that, together with the stabbing action of its canine teeth and its bone-shearing incisors, allow it to overpower much larger prey. A urine scent post on a hard-rubbed elm was another signal to other tigers that this was an established territory. Knowing that such a powerful creature had paused right here in these silent trees, the fire-striped coat rising and falling as it breathed and listened, was exhilarating, to say the least. Besides excellent hearing, tigers have binocular and color vision. In combination with tail lashing, which raises the black tail tuft in warning, a threatened tiger may rotate its ears to show the bold black-ringed white spots on the backs; otherwise their markings have evolved as camouflage adaptations for tall grass, reeds, and woodlands, just as the spots of leopard and jaguar reflect the dappled lights of wind-danced leaves.

Eventually we neared the capture site at the base of a large Tilia, or basswood, tree where the ground was torn up all around and a sapling as thick as a man's arm had been snapped off clean. The snare restricts but does not restrain the tiger's movements, and Lena's captors spoke with awe of the terrible roars and lunging, the ferocity, with which this 252-pound female had made three swift roaring charges on the cable of her snare before being immobilized by two shotgun-fired darts. (Later that year, a large male tiger pulled free of a snare at Dale Miquelle's approach, but fortunately it bounded off without attacking him.)

Since her capture, Lena had moved less than a mile upstream. Doubtless agitated by the contraption on her neck, perhaps still foot-sore or disoriented by the drug, her instinct may have been to remain in hiding in the cool undergrowth. Using rough triangulation to fix her location, we paused at a point that Maurice judged to be no more than a hundred yards from the place where the agitated tiger was switching her long tail in the alders by the brook. At such close quarters, the great head with its broad black nostrils and long, shining whiskers would already be raised and alert, twitching flies from the white-spotted ears, the visage camouflaged in the striped sunlight by the calligraphy of bold black lines inscribed on the white brows and beard and ruff, in that beautiful and terrifying mask of snow and fire.

In *Dersu the Trapper*, Arseniev translates an inscription he had found in a Chinese joss house in Primorski Krai: "To the Lord Tiger who dwelleth in the Forest and the Mountains. In ancient days . . . He saved the state. Today his spirit brings happiness to man." Being so near this agitated tiger, I could scarcely say that her spirit brought me "happiness," yet on this day in the Kunalaika forest while Lena observed us from her place of hiding, I felt a kindled exaltation very close to joy—joy in the sense that word was used by the poet Elizabeth Bishop when confronted with the enigma of a roadside moose:

> *Why, why do we feel*
> *(we all feel) this sweet*
> *sensation of joy?*

Over the receiver came more rapid beeping, indicating that Lena, although not moving away, was up and moving. She did not roar but nobody believed that she was in good temper.

We kept our eyes fixed on the sunny greenwood. The tigress lay down, then rose again and moved in a tight circuit like a caged animal, her restlessness transmitted by her signal. But even knowing we were there, she remained where she had rested for the past three days. Finally we withdrew quietly and left the forest.

One morning, out looking for birds, I went off alone to explore beaches and ponds and bluffs along the coast, keeping a sharp eye out for Amba. Another day, Maurice Hornocker and I went salmon fishing off the coast with Volodya Velichko, the elk hunter and local entrepreneur who had helped in Olga's capture. The sea was clear and clean and the sea-run salmon plentiful. On this beautiful cool summer day, we were pleased to observe two goral on the sea cliffs, and a white-tailed sea eagle watching over all from its guano crag.

Volodya Velichko

In one of those barters that ease a hard and improvised existence in the new Russia, a trawler dumped a cornucopia of fresh sea scallops and octopi into Volodya's boat, to be consumed later at his cheerful cottage with our fresh pink salmon, cucumbers, dark bread, elk venison, and the relentless vodka toasts that stun all visitors to Russia. Since no money changed hands, we supposed that Volodya supplied the fishermen with elk meat, which together with beets and potatoes is the mainstay of the local diet in these hungry times. Elk is also the main prey of the tiger in a landscape where prey animals are sparse, setting up a competition with mankind that the tiger seems doomed to lose.

A few days later, Lena was still in the same location, although she had long since metabolized the drug and should have resumed her hunting circuit. Possibly she had made a fortuitous kill where she was resting, but the biologists worried that something had gone wrong, that she was ill, that a precious animal of a rare species might have been harmed. Since Maurice and I were leaving the next day, we decided to camp at a cabin in the Kunalaika Valley and make a last reconnaissance before first light.

At daybreak, as the woodland birds awakened, we set off with Dale Miquelle into the forest. Following the dim path through wet ferns, tracking her signal, we approached Lena even closer than before, hoping to disturb her just enough to get her moving. Having crowded her as much as we dared, we kept our vigil for an hour. Soon the sun rising from the Sea of Japan burned the coast ridges with bright fire, and the cuckoos and thrushes ceased their singing in the leafy stillness. There was only a woodpecker's solitary tapping—a hollow tap, a waiting silence, then another. *Tap.*

Dersu had told V. K. Arseniev that all Creation was one body, that it was "all same man; also ground, hill, forest . . . all same man. Hear him breathe, all same man." I could feel the tigress breathing as I breathed, and perhaps her sharp eyes could see us through the trees. Certainly she heard us, for her radio signal shifted to a rapid *beep-beep-beep* as she rose and circled. Her harlequin mask would have turned in our direction, the striped fur rising and falling with the fetid meaty breath as she stared and listened—I could all but smell her. Even so, her signal slowed and she settled down again. Perhaps she had been pregnant and had given birth prematurely due to the stress of capture. Perhaps she had made a fortuitous kill and was still guarding it beside the brook—we would never know.

With Maurice Hornocker, I took advantage of a government helicopter departing for Khabarovsk, which would spare us fifteen hours of rough driving. Dale Miquelle, who had a local girlfriend and had learned some Russian, would remain in Terney with Evgeny Smirnov and Igor Nikolaev, who had now been trained to monitor the tiger signals. Our friends would send word of Lena to America.

Departing Terney, the helicopter crossed the yellow-leafed oak forests of Sikhote-Alin, following the ridges north to the Bikin River. East of here, South Korea's Hyundai Corporation had obtained from Russia's Ministry of Forest Industry a thirty-year joint-venture lease on 200,000 acres of virgin forest above the Svetlaya settlement on the Pacific slope. Hyundai (in partnership with Mitsubishi of Japan) had promised meaningful reforestation but, anxious to recoup its investment quickly, had faithfully ignored its promises after finishing the all-out clear-cutting of the spruce-fir forests on the high plateaus. So far it had cut close to 400,000 cubic yards (about 5,000 acres), with three times that amount to be stripped from the mountainsides by the year's end.

In 1995, when this Svetlaya operation was already winding down for want of timber, Siberian Tiger Project scientists made their sole visit to the site, where their Korean hosts offered to sell them a nice tiger skin. Fortunately Hyundai did not cross the ridge into the ancient forest of the pristine Bikin Basin, a 600,000-acre watershed which, together with the Samaga drainage and the zapovedniki, are almost the last virgin forest in Ussuria. The Bikin, 310 miles long, is all but untouched, and the Russian tiger researcher Dimitri Pikunov, a champion of the Udege aborigines who live there, has estimated that its basin contains 10 percent or more of all the Amur tigers left on earth.

The Udege and Nanai peoples of the Bikin drainage trap for furs—mostly sable, otter, squirrel—and subsist largely on meat, but like Dersu, they revere and respect Amba and do not take more of his food than they need, so as not to anger him. In their main settlement at Krasny Yar, there is high feeling against logging, which threatens the tiger and their Tungus culture, too. With support from certain governmental groups as well as environmental organizations, the Udege were doggedly protesting the invasion. But Hyundai maintained a powerful lobby in the regional governments, and the future of the Bikin and its tiger habitat, not to speak of its indigenous human beings, was in deep shadow.

From Khabarovsk, Maurice Hornocker and I traveled by road to the Bolshe Khetskhir Reserve, near the confluence of the Ussuri with the Amur, where we attended an emergency conference of the beleaguered wildlife zapovedniki. As all participants agreed, forest management in the new Russia was utterly demoralized and broke, and income from timber and mining leases to foreign corporations had become critical if the reserves were to survive. Yet these leases were being seriously abused by the headlong multinational corporations, and inevitably the environmental arm of the Ministry of Forestry was a lot less powerful than its branch for forest industry, which with the Moscow government's approval was selling off the future of Siberia at bargain rates. In the words of one weary environmentalist, "The high officials claim that funds have been allocated for the conservation of

the forests, but it invariably turns out that they have not." Most of Siberia was still remote and protected by the lack of roads, but the Amur Basin, accessible to shipping for hundreds of miles upriver, would be destroyed for the huge new markets in Korea and Japan.

U.S. corporations were also descending on Siberia, notably Weyerhaeuser, whose insatiable clear-cutting in the Pacific Northwest of the United States, with accompanying destruction of the rivers, did not bear out a naïve Russian notion that American companies know how to practice forestry. Russia has 58 percent of the world's coniferous forest (the United States 11 percent, Canada 14 percent), according to Weyerhaeuser, which, like many multinational corporations, was mainly interested in rapid exploitation of the Russian Far East and was seeking a lease in the wild region of the Botcha River, north of the Hyundai operation at Svetlaya.

To judge from the Pacific Northwest, where the defenders of the northern spotted owl are ridiculed and threatened in order to distract attention from decades of corporate job-killing practices such as mill automation and the sale of raw timber abroad—and with it all the wood-processing jobs that created the finished products—these global industries would return nothing to the starved local economies. (Hyundai actually arrived with its own workers.) They were far more likely to strip the region of its resources and get out before regulatory apparatus could be put in place that might salvage something of Siberia for Russia's future. Needless to say, an early casualty of rampant logging will be the Amur tiger, which Maurice Hornocker calls "the spotted owl of the Siberian Far East."

Compared to the earth's dwindling rain forests, the great taiga of Siberia has been largely ignored by environmentalists, but it is important from every point of view, not only biodiversity and earth resources but the renewal and health of the planet's precious air and water through absorption of pollutants and production of carbon dioxide. Without intervention and protection, efforts to save very rare species such as the Amur tiger and the Far Eastern leopard will be in vain.

• • •

Khabarovsk, where the Ussuri joins the Amur, is essentially a seaport 500 miles inland from the delta, and also a port of entry on the China border, and its huge bazaar displays in endless racks and stalls the smuggled, stolen, or cheap ersatz Western goods of the engulfing global market. I was happy to leave there early in July with an international ornithological expedition, boarding a ship bound up the Amur as far north and west as Blagovachensk, hunting for nesting grounds of two species of rare cranes. Still on the crane search, I returned south to the Ussuri Valley and Lake Khanka, on my way to Heilongjiang and a third crane expedition to the remote rivers and marshes of eastern Mongolia. All of these regions, with their contiguous regions of northern China, lie within the tiger's former range.

In late summer, returning to America, I found word from Dr. Hornocker that within a few days of our departure from Terney, the tigress Lena had resumed hunting in a normal manner. Since then, a third tigress had been snared and collared. In October we would learn from Dale Miquelle that a fourth female and two half-grown cubs (called Maria Ivanovna, Katerina, and Kolya) had been caught in the north part of the reserve, making six "marked" animals altogether. The Siberian Tiger Project was well under way. Elated, Maurice invited me to return in winter, when there was a far better chance to see a tiger, but three years would pass before this came about.

The resplendent tiger rivals the African elephant and the blue whale as the most majestic and emblematic creature in the folklore and imagination of mankind. But while the elephant and its immense mysteries have been well studied, the tiger, due to its crepuscular and covert habits, has suffered until recent decades from an almost total lack of systematic long-term research in the field. Indeed, by the time the Siberian Tiger Project had commenced, at least three of the eight subspecies or geographic races of *Panthera tigris* presently recognized by the taxonomists were effectively extinct in the wild.

Even the phylogeny of tigers—the evolution and history of the cat family *Felidae* and its tiger species—is only very dimly under-

stood. In the Oligocene, early foxlike animals were evolving into dogs and bears, raccoons and weasels; certain marine bears along the coasts of the Pacific became the ancestors of walruses and the eared seals or "sea lions." Meanwhile, early mongoose relatives were evolving into the hyenas and the cats, including the extinct saber-toothed cats, which were a separate subfamily of the *Felidae*, not closely related to the modern forms.

The *Panthera* genus of big roaring cats includes the tiger and lion, the leopard, and the jaguar; in older texts, the snow leopard is sometimes listed, but most authorities exclude it from *Panthera* because it does not roar. (In the snow leopard the set of throat bones known as the hyoid apparatus is fixed, as in the clouded leopard, mountain lion, and cheetah, rather than cartilaginous and flexible, as in the roaring cats.) Originally the group evolved in response to a great Pleistocene explosion of ungulate animals, in particular the many species of deer, pigs, and wild cattle, which created a clear ecological niche for a large predator that worked the forest borders, and the tiger was likely the earliest modern member of this group to appear. "Molecular phylogenies . . . show that the tiger diverged from the [*Panthera*] ancestor more than two million years ago, before the divergence of the lion, leopard, and jaguar," according to Andrew Kitchener of the Royal National Museum of Scotland, who in recent years has made a painstaking analysis of museum specimens.

The earliest known tiger fossils, dating from the late Pliocene and early Pleistocene, come from localities as far apart as central Java, northern China, and Lyakhov Island, off the north coast of Siberia. The Javan animals were as large as or larger than any modern race, and had already developed the narrower foot found in the modern tigers. However, it is generally believed that this tiger was not the direct ancestor of the modern Javan species, which came later from the mainland, reaching the islands of the Sunda Shelf by way of the land bridges formed by the lowering of oceans in the twenty or more stadials or ice ages that waxed and waned for 1.7 million years during the Pleistocene.

Curiously, the tiger did not follow the great herds across the land bridge called Beringia during the Pleistocene exchange of fauna between Eurasia and North America, possibly because—despite its tolerance of Siberian winters down to −40°F—it could not hibernate like the brown bear and therefore retreated with the onset of the icebound winter, or because the tiger niche in North America had been partially occupied by other cats, including lynx, mountain lion, cheetah, and "saber-toothed tiger." However, late Pleistocene fossils identified as tigers have turned up in eastern Beringia, and so, perhaps, it trailed the elk on summer journeys as far as west Alaska but died out before a breeding population became established. No tiger fossils have turned up in the Americas, nor did the tiger spread west into Europe, perhaps because of competition with the closely related lion.

A "northern theory" of tiger radiation was propounded early by a Russian naturalist and big-game hunter: "There is reason to believe that many of the larger animals such as gaur and buffalo were originally inhabitants of Siberia and Manchuria, and the climatic conditions which were responsible for driving them to the South would undoubtedly account for the tiger accompanying them in search of food."

In recent years, this idea has been contested by another theory that *Panthera tigris* originated in southern China, due to primitive skull characteristics allegedly still present in the so-called South China race, *P. t. amoyensis.* But this China fossil is intermediate in size between a leopard and a small tiger and therefore might be an ancestral leopard, since the roaring cats of the *Panthera* genus are so closely related that lion and tiger skulls are virtually identical, and the leopard skull, too, is indistinguishable except for size. As Kitchener observes, "It is commonly stated that the center of evolution for tigers was northern China but the fossil evidence is equivocal given the wide distribution of the species at the beginning of the Pleistocene. It is also unnecessary to require or even envisage such a restricted locality for the tiger's evolution, since all that is required is sufficient temporal separation of a population to allow its genetic and morphological divergence from a sister or ancestral species, which could have occurred over a wide area of eastern Asia." (In his view, gene flow among tigers has been so extensive until recent times that it is hard to isolate distinct genetic groups, unless it is the Caspian race or the island tigers. In the absence of significant evidence for separating the tiger into different subspecies, he concludes that there may be three at most, and possibly none at all. On the other hand, the diversity of tiger features which distinguish its separate populations usefully points up the wonderful adaptability of the species as a whole.)

At present, most authorities suppose that the species *tigris*, evolving in northeastern Asia when much of the Gobi Desert and arid Central Asia was verdant steppe and Mongolia's rivers were bordered by reed thicket and riverine forest, spread west all the way to the Caucasus and eastern Turkey, where the Caspian tiger, as it is called, would represent the westernmost prong of the expansion. It also moved southward into Southeast Asia and southwest into the Indian subcontinent. When sea levels receded during the Pleistocene to expose or narrow the Sunda Shelf, which linked the Malay peninsula to the East Indies, it crossed to Sumatra, Java, and Bali—presumably before the late Pleistocene, since the mitochondrial DNA type of the island tigers is identical to that of the mainland forms, even though the last land bridge between Sumatra and the Malaysian Peninsula subsided beneath the Malacca Strait approximately eight thousand years ago, before the end of the last ice age.

As the earth warmed after the ice ages, the animals dispersing southward apparently lost their long-haired pelage and heavy tufted paws and huge dimensions: among modern tigers, the only races comparable in size to the primordial tigers are the Siberian and the Indian or Bengal race, both of which have maintained great length and weight in order to deal efficiently with the larger ungulates such as elk in the north and in the south the elk-sized sambar deer. In warmer latitudes, the size of the Pleistocene predator was no longer efficient, since neither the larger heat-producing engine (relative to heat-losing surface) as an adaptation to cold climate nor the size required to bring down huge Pleistocene mammals remained an advantage. (Tiger size corresponds to the size of its main prey, which is generally though not invariably smaller in the tropics and in island fauna.) By the late Pleistocene, the modern tiger was established in a wider distribution than almost any of the cats except the leopard and the lion, from below the equator at 10 degrees south latitude to eastern Siberia at 50 degrees north. Excepting the ellipse of arid mountains and plateaus in the central wastes of the Himalayan rain shadow in the Kunlun Mountains and Tibet, this wonderful animal hunted an astonishing variety of forest habitats, from dry upland woodlands to the raining jungles and the coastal mangrove.

Screens, Nanzen-ji Temple, Kyoto, Japan

During the ebb and flow of the great glaciers, the tiger reached Sakhalin Island and Japan and Borneo (where the Bisaya tribe still prizes its few tiger teeth, claiming that tigers were hunted by their ancestors as recently as two or three centuries ago). In Japan, it apparently went extinct before mankind arrived to finish it, though it survives as a prominent icon and a subject of Japanese art, as in

the bold, strong, delicate draw-
ings of Sengai and the vivid
golden tiger screens in Nanzen-
ji Temple in Kyoto. In the
absence of any fossil record in
Sri Lanka, which was also isolated by the rising seas, it is
supposed that the tiger may
have arrived on the Indian
subcontinent rather late—too
late to reach Sri Lanka during
the lowering of oceans—though
here again, as in Beringia, it
might have arrived there only
to die out.

With the coming of man's
agriculture and settled villages, the clearing of the for-
ests was well under way, and over the millennia, the regional tiger
populations were gradually cut off from one another. Since the tiger
adapted so readily to different climates, the disparity in ecological
conditions would eventually produce populations more or less distinct
in size, stripe patterns, and coloration—sufficient rough criteria in
the early days of Linnaean taxonomy for identification as a morphological "subspecies," or race.

All modern cats—there are thirty-seven species—are closely
related, differing mainly in response to prey size and camouflage requirements. As the most strictly carnivorous of terrestrial mammals,
for example, all felids share the intense focus on hunting that is no-

Universal feline behaviors— flehmen, groom-ing, play-fighting, spraying—in Amur tigers

ticed at once in the activities of cubs and kittens—stalking and rac-
ing, pouncing and grasping is their only play. Indeed, so similar in
their ethology are most of the large cats—exceptions might be the
open-country lion and the cheetah—that much of what is known or
at least supposed about tiger behavior in the wild has been inferred
from the behavior of the tiger's smaller relatives.

Whatever the genetic validity of tiger sub-
species or geographic races, the Amur population, *P. t. altaica*, is generally represented as the largest of the modern tigers. While it is true
that in its winter pelage, *altaica*—once called *longipilis* due to its
long hair—appears more massive than the Indian race, it is only two
to four inches taller at the shoulder than those mighty Bengal tigers,
P. t. tigris, from the northern subcontinent under the Himalayas.
Though large males of both races may range from nine to twelve feet
in length, *altaica*, which must hunt harder and more widely for its
food, may actually weigh less: Igor Nikolaev, the Siberian Tiger Project researcher with most experience in the field, knows of no wild
Amur tiger that has exceeded 650 pounds, a weight claimed also for
P. t. tigris. Theoretically, a large wild female might reach 450 pounds,
but as of 1999, the project has weighed some fifteen tigresses without finding one larger than about 320. (Sexual dimorphism is pronounced in the larger races, in which the male may weigh up to
1.7 times as much as the female; the reasons for this are not well understood.) In any case, the average weights recorded by the project
seem to be lower than those noted in the past. (At least one authority

Panthera tigris altaica (adult female)

suspects this is the difference between real weights and hunters' estimates, pointing out that tigers live perhaps fifteen years in the wild and twenty or more in captivity, and ordinarily keep growing all their lives, and that therefore truly enormous males occasionally appear among all of the big cats, including jaguars and mountain lions.)

While all tigers are essentially the same animal, size tends to diminish in a cline as the species radiates toward the equator. Thus the South China, Indochinese, and Caspian races (*P. t. amoyensis*, *corbetti*, and *virgata*) are reportedly smaller than *altaica*, and the three island races of the tropics—the Sumatran, Javan, and Bali tigers (*P. t. sumatrae*, *sondaica*, and *balica*) are smaller still. (The extinct Japanese form was approximately the same size as the island tigers.) Even in southern India, *P. t. tigris* is not only smaller but darker and more densely striped than the large *tigris* farther north, like the tigers of Southeast Asia and the islands.

The marking above each tiger's eye is as unique as a human fingerprint

Wherever the species occurs, the tiger resides at the summit of its ecosystem, and the health of the tiger population is the best indicator of the health of the ecosystem as a whole. By regulating the herbivore populations through predation, the tiger ensures stability and biodiversity for the whole system; it is also what ecologists call an "umbrella species," the protection of which shelters and conserves other plant and animal forms as natural resources.

Although much hunted and reduced, *Panthera tigris* maintained its abundance as late as the turn of the present century, when by common estimate, 100,000 tigers still survived. Since then its decline has been precipitous. "No doubt the species is now on its way to extinction," one authority would observe more than fifty years ago. Three of its geographic populations, perhaps four, have been extinguished in my lifetime, and at least three others may vanish forever in the first decades of the new century. Given the hardihood and tenacious adaptability of this species, such a calamity is profoundly saddening. Even as it disappears, information and data on the status and distribution of the tiger's surviving races remains surprisingly incomplete—a sign in itself of how little is known about this dangerous hunter.

Present estimates of tiger numbers in the wild range between 4,600 and 7,700. A Wildlife Conservation Society (WCS) report in November 1995 proposed a total of "less than 5,000" and most biologists and conservationists I have spoken with in the course of tiger travels would set that number even lower. Certainly one cannot accept the official figures of Asia's "tiger range states," which for various political reasons continue to claim ghostly tigers in battered landscapes where no viable population could subsist.

In almost all the tiger states, the forces acting to obliterate the species are depressingly alike, though the order of impact differs from country to country. Near-invariable factors are the destruction and loss of habitat due to ever-increasing human presence and activity, including agriculture, lumbering and mining, forest fires, and war; also, the hunting and poaching of the tiger and its prey, which in turn increases livestock predation and fatal confrontations with man; "inbreeding depression" (low gene variation in tigers too closely related, leading to poor immunity to disease and/or low fertility, therefore high mortality, and finally extinction of that group); and "genetic drift"—in effect, a condition caused by random loss of genes in small populations. Though specific events that put an end to the last individuals in a population are rarely known, it was probably inevitable that the first geographic races to disappear were the Balinese (last reliable sighting or report in 1939), Caspian (1968), and Javan (1979) populations, which had probably been separated longest from the main body of the species and which died out at the farthest east-west outposts of the tiger's range.

The Caspian (or Turan or Hyrcanian) tiger was always separated from its kin on the Indian subcontinent by the high desert ranges of Afghanistan and northern Pakistan; in recent millennia, as the forests contracted and the great steppe dried and turned to desert, *P. t. virgata* became isolated from the tigers of eastern Asia by the widening barrier of dry plateaus in north Mongolia, Sinkiang, and north Tibet and the cold wastes of the Kunlun Mountains and the Taklamakan Desert. ("Taklamakan" means something like "He who enters there does not come out.") The tiger can tolerate the cold, but it cannot survive in arid country where even its prey may have difficulty finding food and water.

P. t. virgata was a medium-sized, pale tiger (its stripes were said to be brownish rather than black) of the reed beds of the Caucasus and the great inland seas of western Asia. We know it best as that scowling palace skulker depicted since early times in Persian art. (To my ear, "Persia" seems more exotic than "Iran," therefore more suitable as a haunt of tigers.) It ranged formerly from eastern Turkey and the northern borders of Iran and Afghanistan to the south shores of the Caspian and Aral Seas, east to Lake Balkhash and Kazakhstan in Central Asia, possibly as far as the western border of Mongolia. Within this vast and mostly arid range, it had a limited distribution along the lakeshores and small river valleys—inevitably the first locations settled with the coming of man. Therefore it is thought to have been bolder in its dispersal than the southern

Royal hunt, Persian miniature, 1554

tigers, moving greater distances and even crossing dry and open country in search of man-free territory. An interesting reference from the 1920s notes, "The small species [of southwest Siberia] which is short-haired and rather smudgily striped has his headquarters in the swampy flats around Lake Balkash in the southwest, though he ranges eastward, just south of the Altasin [Altai] Mountains, in fairish numbers, all the way to China."

In Iran as elsewhere, the tiger received official protection before it vanished but the laws were ineffectually enforced. Although "the small tiger found in southwest Siberia" was rarely shot, "poisoned bait . . . is laid in his haunts during the winter when his skin is in fine condition and fetches a big price [with] Chinese middlemen who smuggle furs out through Manchuria."

In any case, the race was doomed by the destruction of the native forest and the deer species, which were never abundant and were always heavily hunted. Along the south shore of the Caspian, malaria control brought a sudden increase in the human population, and in Kazakhstan, the burning of the dense reed thickets in the river valleys by steppe fires destroyed much of the marsh habitat used by deer and boar. Similarly, in Turkmenia, excessive hunting, in combination with the clearing of the dense *tugai* vegetation for new cotton fields in the region of the Aral Sea, may have eliminated a last breeding population.

In 1964, two tigers were killed near Lenkoran, on the southwest shore of the Caspian near the Iran border—quite possibly the animals mentioned a few years later by a British travel writer: "In Baku there had been talk of tigers and other exotic fauna and flora in the hinterland of Lenkoran . . . Was it not here or hereabouts . . . that Tamerlane himself hunted the tiger?" Since then, Baku has all but disappeared in the gargantuan apparatus of its oil fields and refineries, and the last good tiger habitat may have vanished with it.

In the early 1970s, an American researcher who surveyed Iran's Caspian shore with camera traps found leopard sign but no evidence of tiger, and a mountain survey in Iran between 1973 and 1976 had the same result. Today the Caspian tiger is presumed extinct.

On research expeditions in 1990, 1992, and 1996, I visited tiger reserves in India and the Russian Far East, as well as certain locations of the tiger's former range, such as Lake Baikal, Bali, South Korea, south-central China, and the remote rivers and marshes of eastern Mongolia. Today most of these regions are devoid of tigers, though a few may persist across the Russian border in northeastern China and in the mountains of northeastern North Korea.

Formerly identified as *P. t. coreensis*, "the Korean tiger," this relict population is no longer recognized as distinguishable from the Amur race, far less as "smaller, much darker and more fully striped [with] a shorter less woolly winter coat," as it was described in the Red Data Book of the Convention on International Trade in Endangered Species (CITES) as recently as 1965. According to that excellent publication, which lists all species thought to be endangered, an estimated 200 *coreensis* survived in China, with thirty or forty more in North Korea.

Twenty years ago, Dr. Ma Yiquing, an ebullient and optimistic Chinese field biologist whom I met on that crane expedition up the

Amur River, had estimated 150 "Manchurian" tigers in the mountains of northeastern China, about eighty of these in Heilongjiang and seventy in Jilin. Such an estimate was surely optimistic even in 1979, because the following year, Maurice Hornocker, denied permission to work in the Soviet Union, traveled to the Hu Lin region of Heilongjiang in the hope of working with these tigers, only to discover that the last good habitat was all but gone and that what was left was rapidly disappearing in ill-advised timbering projects. In fact, tiger prospects in northeastern China seemed so hopeless even then that he abandoned the idea and returned home. Today it appears very unlikely that the last *altaica* south and west of the Russian border can amount to more than twenty animals altogether.

The situation is no better and probably somewhat worse in North Korea, although the Paektu Mountain region on the Jilin border, about 67 miles north and south and 50 miles east and west, seems to contain suitable habitat for tigers. In late January 1996, on a crane survey along the Demilitarized Zone (DMZ) between the two Koreas, I discussed tigers with naturalist Kim Sooil, an environmental biologist at the Korean National University and an advisor to the Ministry of the Environment. Dr. Kim assured me that although both tiger and leopard had formerly been plentiful throughout the Korean peninsula, the last confirmed tiger record in South Korea had been made in 1942, and the last leopards had been poisoned out after the Korean War. There were rumors that a few leopards persisted in the heavily mined and fiercely monitored DMZ—where we found small roe deer abundant along the boundaries—but nobody had dared enter to find out.

Dr. Kim's parents had been born near Pyongyang, North Korea, where "the mountain water held the ginseng's essence." His mother had told him that tigers were quite common in the countryside during her girlhood, and that on several occasions, returning from market after dark, the produce cart on which she rode had been followed by a tiger, which the farmers would scare off by throwing torches of burning hay. Though Dr. Kim put no credence in North Korea's recent claim to about ten tigers said to be living in the vicinity of Mt. Paektu in the far northeast, a recent report allegedly based on foot surveys and research interviews in 2,300 square miles of Lyangan Province in that region "verified the existence of tigers . . . Sufficient numbers of tiger tracks were found in the area to conclude that a large number of tigers inhabit this region. Survey results . . . showed an abundance of prey resources."

The new North Korea survey was facilitated by the Siberian Tiger Project's Igor Nikolaev and Dimitri Pikunov. As Dale Miquelle commented in a letter of July 1999, "Representatives of [the North Korean] Institute of Geography insist that populations of tiger reside in several patches of habitat, including one close to the DMZ," and he and his colleagues would take advantage of every opportunity to survey those regions. Their great hope was to find an "ecological corridor" which would link the Primorski Krai tigers through a sliver of habitat in China with a remnant North Korean population.

The Korean people are of Chinese stock, mixed racially and linguistically with the Tungus-speaking tribes and the Mongolians, and they share with Dersu's Tungus peoples of the Amur watershed a belief in the beneficent aspects of the tiger. The Mun Bae tiger, which protects the household from evil, is a common icon, not ferocious like most guardians but on the contrary a friendly, naïve creature easily fooled by magpies and such tricksters. In Korea, too, the tiger is represented as the peaceful companion of a wise old sage known as "the

Mountain Spirit," for whom it serves as a sacred messenger of harmony and peace.

Hanging scroll, Korea, eighteenth century

The South China or Amoy tiger, *P. t. amoyensis,* was formerly abundant in subtropical and temperate upland forests from the Yellow Sea all the way west to the upper Yangtze and Huang Ho watersheds. It is said to be smaller and darker than *altaica,* with less extensive white on the underside. As late as the 1940s and early 1950s, before forest clearing for agriculture destroyed most of its habitat and tiger harvest for the government became a significant source of income in mountainous regions, its population was estimated (by the Chinese) at about 4,000 tigers. But ongoing loss of habitat to settlement, together with increased public access to firearms, sadly reduced the tiger's prey, a situation followed here as elsewhere by reports of increased tiger predation on livestock and human beings. In 1959, under Mao Tse-tung, the tiger was officially condemned as an enemy of man, and organized eradication campaigns against these "pests" were encouraged by government bounties, intensifying local hunting not only for the pelts but for the growing market in tiger bones, blood, and organs used in traditional medicines. By the early 1960s, *amoyensis* had declined to an estimated 1,000 animals, and a decade later, even the Chinese could agree that "the tiger is now extremely scarce in China" and that without serious conservation efforts "the Chinese tiger will shortly become extinct."

Though tigers were occasionally reported from rural regions of east, central, and south China, and west up the river valleys as far as Szechwan and Kansu, the tiger's range was now essentially restricted to three isolated areas of southern China. Two of these regions were in Jiangxi Province, south of the Yangtze River. In the winter of 1993, traveling from Hong Kong to Nanchang, I flew north and south over this province at low altitude and in clear weather, which permitted an extended view of the scarred landscape of low battered mountains on all sides. I also drove overland for five hours north and east, from Nanchang to the Poyang Lakes. To judge from the stunning extent of man-made destruction seen from the roads as well as from the air, the last redoubts of the tiger in Jiangxi were dangerously imperiled at the very least.

Officially, about one hundred *amoyensis* are still surviving in the wild, but to judge from the condition of Jiangxi, I could scarcely believe that more than twenty or thirty were left, and even this figure seemed optimistic, since no one seems to have reported any recent sightings. In a letter of April 1996, tiger authority Dr. John Seidensticker, curator of mammals at Washington's National Zoo, commented, "I, too, have trouble believing there are even twenty *amoyensis*." At present, about fifty specimens are said to survive in China's zoos, and theoretically these animals could serve as a genetic nucleus for resurrecting the Chinese tiger, but it seems more likely that this race will become the fourth to vanish in my lifetime, if in fact it has not already done so.

The most recent subspecies to be recognized by the taxonomists is the Indochinese tiger, *P. t. corbetti*, which came into existence (on paper, at least) in 1968, or about the time that *P. t. coreensis* was stricken from the list. It is said to have a deeper ground color, with more numerous, rather short and narrow stripes.

Bronze belt buckle, Chinese (800–400 B.C.), Dion culture

This population is widely scattered throughout Southeast Asia, from eastern Myanmar (the former Burma) throughout the former Indochina—Thailand, Laos, Vietnam, Cambodia, and Malaysia—with occasional wanderers into southern China. It is said to be slightly smaller than *amoyensis*, with which it may have interbred along the Myanmar and Laos borders, thus maintaining a clinal variation toward the south that is indicated by darker pelage and closer striping.

However, Dr. Alan Rabinowitz of WCS, who has surveyed *corbetti* and its range since 1993, says it would be difficult to find a "pure" *corbetti* even if such a creature existed; from all measurements he has been able to locate in the hunters' reports and other sources which he has gathered from all over Southeast Asia, he is unable to find any good evidence that it differs in any way from the Indian tiger. "The overall body sizes are just the same in both male and female, even the paw size and track measurements; the only difference indicated was that it might be a little bit leaner!"

Estimates of *corbetti* numbers range from 1,400 to over 2,000, but due to the huge and little-known forests in its war-torn terrain, its actual status is less clear than that of other tiger populations; in fact, there is a woeful lack of substantiated data from any of these countries of the former Indochina. Speculating that its numbers may have increased due to food supplied to it in the form of war dead, one writer cites "a Vietnam veteran, Major A. D. Ackels, who reported that tigers had been seen scavenging corpses, in addition to occasional attacks on soldiers." (All the larger cats except the cheetah, which feeds only one time from its kill, are known to resort to carrion on occasion.) Assuming that such accounts are true, any dietary benefit to the tigers was offset long ago by the chronic failure to control the hunting, snaring, and trapping of all wildlife, resulting in very low prey densities even where disturbed forest still exists. The local people have no say in forest management, nor do they benefit from game protection, which merely denies them a traditional source of protein.

In Myanmar, where 45 percent of the country remains forested, scarcely 1 percent is now protected. Alaungdaw Kathapa National Park, its largest reserve, claims Asian elephant, Himalayan bear, sun bear, and clouded leopard, but as in almost all these

Vietnamese folk art

countries, conservation laws, when they exist, are rarely implemented. Even where chronic civil war has not driven the forest guards out of the forests, they have no authority to arrest poachers. Beset by a brutal military dictatorship and civil strife, environmental disasters, isolation, and cruel poverty, Myanmar is riddled with poaching and smuggling together with the illegal logging of its valuable teak forest. According to Rabinowitz, who has done surveys there since 1993, the tiger's best hope may be Hkakaborazi National Park, a 1,500-square-mile tract in the far north, in Kachin.

Thailand, at the heart of *corbetti*'s range, is the only Indochinese country that has had the benefit of substantive research. In the nineteenth century, Thailand was noted for its abundant tigers, and they were still plentiful as late as the 1950s; soon after that, hundreds of tiger skins started to turn up in Bangkok tourist shops. Since then, the country's forests have declined more than 70 percent, and Thailand is no longer a major exporter of tropical wood, which it must now import. The only near-pristine forests left lie within the national parks and wildlife sanctuaries, but even these are confusingly administered by several different government departments.

In 1972 the tiger finally received protection, and trade in live animals and tiger products was prohibited, but large villages lie within the protected areas, causing the usual forest degradation from fires, roads, logging, military activity, and agricultural clearing. Dams and reservoirs have destroyed extensive areas of the riverine habitat preferred by the tiger and its prey, and in these regions, the deer and wild boar populations are all but gone. Throughout Thailand, field personnel are few, funding is meager, and conservation all but nonexistent. The ill-paid guards are imperiled by well-armed poachers and even by the local people, who perceive them as adversaries out to interfere with their traditional harvests in the forest.

As wildlife biologist George Schaller of WCS has said, local people have set snares "from the mountain-top all the way down into the valley," and Dr. Rabinowitz agrees. "The people are literally wiping out everything—sambar, barking deer, even young elephants. The forests look good but there are no tigers because there is nothing to eat. In these countries it is not the tiger that is being killed directly but the prey."

On the other hand, Thailand, more than any other tiger state in Southeast Asia, has an existing system of protected areas, staffed and funded, where most of its tigers are already sheltered. In 1995, the Royal Forest Department initiated a tiger restoration project, beginning with a study of the location, size, and degree of isolation in a group of related tiger populations, also prey abundance, habitat condition, the impact of the human population, and other factors. Also, many parks and sanctuaries adjoin one another in a single ecological and administrative unit; the largest of these is the Western Forest Complex, including the Huai Kha Khaeng/Thung Yai World Heritage site—twelve parks and sanctuaries in one unit of 6,118 square miles, which is thought to be capable of supporting about 180 breeding adults. Better still—since this forest complex and four other tiger regions adjoin additional large areas of habitat in Myanmar, Cambodia, and Malaysia—"the trans-boundary tiger populations along the border with Myanmar provide an opportunity to conserve tigers within the largest natural ecosystem in mainland South and Southeast Asia." The largest tiger populations in Thailand and elsewhere tend to occur in border areas—not surprising when one considers that natural barriers such as river systems and mountainous regions often include unsettled wilderness—and so there exist important possibilities for international reserves and parks. The six largest populations include three-quarters of Thailand's total, which is presently estimated at 500 animals.

Laos and Cambodia are poor countries which have retained much of their forest, but wildlife reserve areas are few and conservation all but nonexistent. Like Myanmar, these states have failed to support recommendations made by CITES, and not until 1989 were Laos's tigers granted legal protection. This has done them very little good, to judge from the open marketing of tiger parts in Vientiane.

Due to incessant civil war, little is known about the mountain forests on the borders of these Southeast Asian countries, and the discovery in recent years of several large mammals such as the rare wild ox known as the kouprey have raised hope of undiscovered tiger populations. In April 1999, a report from Cambodia in the *Sunday Times* of London described "a comprehensive survey" which revealed that 700 tigers might inhabit a remote area on the northern border where the presence of about 200 had been inferred before. What was not clear was whether or not this paradisal region was the Virachey Reserve on the Laos–Vietnam border, which lies at the heart of a vast and undisturbed tropical forest of some 30,000 square miles (about the size of Maine). "Despite thirty years of jungle warfare and the pressure from local villagers and soldiers, who use homemade landmines to kill them," the article stated, "the endangered tigers managed to reproduce in jungles where warfare had ensured that development stood still." Now that the dissolution of Pol Pot's Khmer Rouge has lessened the ever-present threat of landmines, it went on, "many remote jungle areas have become accessible for the first time." However, this good news is premature, with no hard data to support it. The habitat appears intact, but whether there are ungulates enough to feed 700 tigers is another matter.

In peninsular Malaysia, most of the remaining jungle is known as "reserve forest," which in practice seems to mean "reserved for logging." As elsewhere, lip service is paid to the recommendations of CITES and the IUCN (the International Union for the Conservation of Nature), but enforcement is negligible. Most of the reserves are wide open to human settlement and exploitation, and there is no control of firearms. Possibly the local people hold to the traditional belief that the tiger's spirit will abide long after it disappears; according to an old Malay saying, "The tiger dies but his stripes remain."

In former times, tigers were rarely hunted even by the few equipped to do so, due to the animist belief throughout Southeast Asia and the islands that all creatures had souls and that man and tiger are soul brothers. The idea of metempsychosis, or soul-transfer, was also pervasive, and tiger-spirits, were-tigers, and tiger shamans (analogous to the leopard shamans of West Africa and the jaguar shamans of the Amazon basin) made certain that this ever-changing creature was much feared as well as worshipped. Use of its name was disrespectful and was generally avoided: it was called "the Striped One" (or, among the Moi of Vietnam, "the Gentleman"). It killed only villagers who broke taboos, for otherwise it might be killed itself. In 1974, a tiger destroyed twenty-four people in a village in northern Burma; after soldiers killed it, the Lisu tribesmen gathered around its head, chanting a prayer of regret and concluding with an entreaty to the tiger that it rest in peace.

Farther south on the peninsula, the tigers grow progressively smaller and darker, so much so that the population southeast of the Isthmus of Kra may have more affinities with the island tigers which long ago crossed an exposed or much narrowed Malacca Strait to inhabit the mountainous western islands of Indonesia such as Sumatra. (The original tiger habitat, perhaps, was the great swamps that are known to have formed between the islands.) Here the tiger appeared as the largest predator in a tropical forest community in which terrestrial animals such as deer were few by comparison to the arboreal primates, for which the leopard was far better adapted. The disappearance of tigers from nearby Borneo—a very large island with ample tiger habitat—may be accounted for in part by the absence of deer, which were introduced relatively recently by man.

Sumatra, bisected by the equator, is the world's sixth-largest island, with mountains and volcanoes, coastal plains, rivers, swamps, jungle, and mangrove. Until recent years, little was known about its tigers because of the remote and vast extent of its all but impenetrable jungles, but by 1940, the island was producing a third of the world's rubber. Its poor soils slowed agricultural settlement until after World War II, but ever since, the conversion of forest land, easily accessible from the slow jungle rivers, has been greatly expanded by rubber and oil palm plantations, timber concessions, and oil fields. Fragmentation of tiger habitat was well under way, and such large reserves as were set aside were mainly in marginal tiger country in mountain rain forests in the north and the southwest. That these were among the last habitats in Asia still remote enough to discourage human access was their foremost virtue.

The Sumatran tiger was well distributed over an island 620 miles long by 185 miles wide—almost as large as the remaining range of the Amur tiger, except that the Sumatran's territory is broken into seven sections, while *altaica*'s is virtually continuous. Though known

66   Peter Matthiessen

to have declined in recent decades, *P. t. sumatrae* was not seriously endangered until after World War II, when the trade in tiger parts was added to accelerating loss of habitat and other factors. As in Thailand, hunting for tiger skins became popular; officially, registered tiger remains included 600 stuffed specimens in government offices and private homes, in addition to the many hundreds being exported.

In Indonesia, the Muslims believe that Allah empowered the tiger to protect the faithful and to mete out punishment to anyone who dares transgress the laws of Islam; "Fearing [that] the tiger is a spirit sent by Allah to punish them," as one Javan writer has observed, "the villagers are driven to purge their conscience of deep buried secrets and past misdeeds in their desperation to survive." On the other hand, a Muslim holy man may ride astride a tiger as blithely as the Taoist sage Chang Tao-ling in his quest for enlightenment, or the goddess Durga in the Indus Valley civilizations, or the Buddhist ancestor Manjusri. But here as elsewhere, the old ways were dying and a new generation, acquiring the values of the West, had little compunction about killing tigers and selling skins and parts to Chinese middlemen. Shipped to Singapore, a well-tanned skin might bring $2,000.

As the decline of tigers everywhere became apparent, the demand for tiger parts grew swiftly, especially in those prosperous states of the Pacific Rim that called themselves "the Asian tigers." Between 1975 and 1992, 8,200 pounds of dried tiger bone from Indonesia—in effect, Sumatra and the Malay Peninsula—were imported by South Korea alone, an amount that represents an estimated 338 to 620 tigers. Between 1991 and 1993, when the tiger was already disappearing, South Korea imported more than a thousand pounds of bone, or about twenty tigers every year. A survey between 1972 and 1975 had arrived at the figure of approximately a thousand tigers living on Sumatra, though there seems to have been no realistic basis for a fair estimate. Within a few years, in any case, the ravages of poaching had become apparent. A total of 400 were now thought to inhabit the five main reserves, with perhaps another hundred wandering the second-growth forest, grassland, and plantation edges. In the largest of the reserves, Gunung Lauser, a complex of about 3,125 square miles in the northern mountains, there were said to be from twenty to a hundred tigers.

These numbers, far too round to be dependable, cannot be much more than inspired guesswork. At a conservation workshop in 1992, "about thirty-five professional Indonesian forestry and conservation officials assigned to Sumatran parks and protected areas—the majority of the tiger professionals in Sumatra—were asked how many had ever laid eyes on a wild tiger. Four raised their hands. How many had seen tiger tracks? Perhaps half of them. How many with raised hands had seen tracks ten or more times? Half the hands went down." Since tigers travel commonly on tracks and dirt roads where their mighty pugmarks are highly visible, this poll was even more ominous than it appeared.

The Sumatran tiger, like the rest, was rapidly succumbing to habitat loss and fragmentation and an ever-decreasing prey base, a plight made worse by the ever-present threat of an ungulate disease that could decimate the small Sumatran deer; already the ungulates as primary food had been augmented by a primate known as the pig-tailed macaque, since the flexible tiger will eat almost anything it can catch. Meanwhile, increasing livestock depredations were leading to fatal encounters with another primate, *Homo sapiens.* In 1979, a provincial police report recorded the astounding news that more people—thirty—had been killed by tigers than had perished at the hands of their own species. In general, tiger attacks upon people and their livestock have been comparatively uncommon in Sumatra—one fatality in the past ten years in the environs of Way Kambas National Park in southeastern Sumatra, despite a population of a half million human beings in the nearby villages (somewhat less than the deaths caused by automobiles and poisonous snakes), but the incidence has increased in several regions, with at least eight mortalities in 1996–97 alone.

As if habitat and prey loss weren't enough, *sumatrae* is beset by the difficulty of finding mates in a small population that is sparsely scattered over the whole island. Also, because its local populations are so small and isolated, it may be afflicted by inbreeding depression, in addition to guns and traps and poisoned baits. For several years poison was used extensively along the forest edge of Gunung Lauser Park, where a leading poacher made the claim that between 1986 and 1994, he had personally destroyed no fewer than fifty tigers.

At a 1991 meeting of the IUCN Cat Specialist group (which at present includes almost all of the tiger authorities cited in this book), the Sumatran tiger was declared to be in "critical" condition; a subsequent report was to conclude that in the continuing absence of serious protection efforts in Sumatra, "there may be no tigers or wilderness left to protect in the year 2000." On the other hand, a field report in 1997 stated that the tigers in Way Kambas "seemed to be flourishing," although only seven of its sixty-odd forestry field staff had ever seen one. Since Way Kambas is small—which increases the exposure of both tigers and prey animals to hunters—this optimism is in part attributable to that park's excellent and dedicated staff, a very uncommon asset in Southeast Asia.

In the end, alas, the long-term survival of *sumatrae* may be fatally threatened by the island's human population of 180 million, which has the potential to double within thirty years—an increase from 6 million to 360 million in a single century. And all these new people naturally aspire to a higher standard of living that can only exhaust Sumatra's environment still further.

In the opinion of John Seidensticker, who has worked with *sumatrae* in the field, special attention must be concentrated on one or two large, promising reserves where tigers and their prey might be sheltered from the all-engulfing pressure of the human species. The best hope for the tigers, he believes, lies in the center of the island on alluvial plains—the peneplains—which extend like fingers into the great swamps; it is urgent that some of this region be set aside before it is irreversibly developed. However, much of the disturbed forest encroached upon by human beings supports more wild boar and deer than many of the reserves, which are often marginal habitat with low prey density. Way Kambas has been cut over at least three times and is surrounded on three sides by heavy human settlement, yet it continues to support a high population of large animals, including what may be the last Sumatran rhinos. Since the last tigers are so widely scattered on the island, forestry management over a wide area must ensure that ungulates are present in sufficient density for tigresses to find food for their young without abandoning the litter for too long while they are hunting. What must be avoided at all costs, Dr. Seidensticker feels, is the scattered administration of tiger lands by competing bureaucracies; and what must be established as soon as possible is the livelihood, welfare, and participation of the local farmers and herdsmen who live near the reserves and who must be persuaded that tiger conservation measures will eventually benefit the tiger's neighbors, too. Without the support of local people, who include the hunters and the poachers, even the most dedicated efforts to protect the future of the Sumatran tiger are bound to fail.

It is said in Java that the tiger's hearing is so acute that hunters must keep their nose hairs cut lest the tiger hear their breath whistle through their nostrils; it is also known that the tiger's strength is supernatural. In the days when tigers were pitted against banteng bulls to titillate the Dutch administrators and other Westerners, the banteng usually thwarted death out of sheer heft and

Javan tigers in the Berlin zoo, early 1900s

bullheadedness, but all the same, the tiger could bring it down. Bounding up alongside from behind and grasping the throat of the big animal, then bracing its legs and twisting the beast's head sideways and back, it rolled the bull over with the force of its own momentum. Though it could not always finish the job, the tiger was able to haul down an animal of 1,800 pounds, at least six times the weight of *P. t. sondaica*.

In Java, the word for tiger is *macan* (Sanskrit) or *harimau* (Malay). However, such names are not used outside the village, in the tiger's own domain; in the jungle, he is *nenek*, which signifies something like "Grandfather" or "Old Man of the Forest," analogous to the guardian spirit in the Tungus-Manchu culture. Yet despite its spiritual significance, the once-abundant Javan tiger, distinctive in its numerous thin stripes, was bountied and poisoned and killed as an agricultural scourge throughout the nineteenth and early twentieth centuries (as was, later, its main prey, the wild pig), and not until the 1920s and 1930s was a system of reserves established to protect it. By that time, most of the monsoon forest had been converted to teak, rubber, and cotton plantations (all of it depauperate as wildlife habitat). Java's human population had already reached 42 million, and today the island is aswarm with 84 million people, rivaling another tiger country, Bangladesh, as one of the world's most densely populated places. Such a virulent increase in human beings, with the devouring of the forests, doomed *sondaica*. The few captive animals in Indonesian and Berlin zoos were dispersed during World War II, and no known descendants seem to have survived. After the war, wild *sondaica* were rare; it was easier to acquire Sumatrans for the zoo collections.

By 1945, *P. t. sondaica* was mostly gone from all but the most remote parts of the island. Though sadly reduced by hunting and poi-soning by irate herders in and around the Ujung Kulon reserve in the west, and also by the severe reduction (by disease) of a critical prey species, the rusa deer, the main cause of its extirpation was loss of habitat, which eventually limited its distribution to small isolated re-serves no longer bulwarked by large forest tracts. By the mid-1960s, when civil unrest spread across the island, *sondaica* survived in only three of those reserves, which also sheltered armed bands of hungry rebels. As late as 1968, at least twelve tigers survived in Ujong Kulon, but despite the near-absence of human beings, these tigers had van-ished less than ten years later. As for Meru-Betiri, a rugged mountain rain forest that descends to the Indian Ocean on the southeast coast, it was "essentially an island surrounded and disrupted by shifting culti-vation and plantations" by the time it was set aside in the 1970s. Mountain rain forests do not support dense ungulate populations—riverine forest and native grassland would have been the tiger's opti-mum habitat in Java—and inevitably, the tiger's prospects were diminished by low prey biomass and high seasonal fluctuations in prey numbers.

"Meru-Betiri and the Javan tiger," as war hero Julius Tahija said in arguing the tiger's case to President Suharto, "are a part of In-donesia's national heritage in the same way that the temples of Borobudur and Prambanan represent our cultural heritage. These monuments are unique and once destroyed cannot be replaced, so no-body is likely to propose their removal to make way for a cement factory, a housing complex, or some other form of development. Yet living natural monuments such as the tiger are similarly both unique and an irreplaceable part not only of our national heritage but that of mankind as a whole."

In 1979, Suharto proposed to relocate 5,000 people from the rubber plantations on the borders of Meru-Betiri, to help protect the reserve's remaining four tigers; since this grandiose idea came much too late, it seems just as well that it was voted down. The fate of those last four *sondaica* is not known. John Seidensticker located tracks of at least three individuals in Meru-Betiri in 1976, and a man affiliated with World Wildlife Fund–Indonesia found a single track in 1979. But an intensive survey by WWF in October of that year found nothing, "and subsequently, all their camera traps produced were leopards. So I think one can date the extinction of *sondaica* to 1979."

The wet, tropical forest vegetation that is typical of the Greater Sunda Islands was always meager habitat for ungulates, and the Bali tiger, with the smallest *cervus* prey, was apparently the smallest of them all. (Reputedly, an adult male *balica* was less than eight feet long.) Reduced size, of course, was no disadvantage in dense tropical jungle with a larger biomass of monkeys than of ungulates; this may partly explain why leopards thrive where tigers do not, as in Sri Lanka and Borneo. (The Asian leopard occurs in Java, but its niche is occupied in Sumatra and Borneo by the clouded leopard, a smaller species of a different genus, *Neofelis*.)

Rich volcanic soil encouraged an intensive wet-rice agriculture on the slopes of eastern Bali, and by 1912 (when its occurrence was first reported), the Bali tiger had already withdrawn to the high mountain forests in the west. There appears to be no record of a specimen of *P. t. balica* captured alive and displayed in a zoo, and only a few skins and scraps from which DNA can be extracted have survived. Nonetheless, its status as a distinct race has been asserted by the Czech taxonomist Vratislav Mazak, who discovered certain cranial variations—for example, a narrower occipital plane—that theoretically distinguish it from the Java tiger.

John Seidensticker, for one, has certain doubts. The hard-hunted Java tiger, after all, could have crossed the mile-wide channel to Bali without difficulty; tigers in the Ganges delta are known to navigate tidal rivers that are far wider, while others have crossed the Amur River on international peregrinations between China and Russia, and also the strait between Singapore and the Malaysian mainland. The tiger is a mighty swimmer, known to have traveled up to eighteen miles across rivers and deltas and nine miles in the sea.

In any case, the collection of museum specimens from *balica*'s small population hastened its extinction, and the Bali Barat Game Reserve, created in 1941, came far too late. In the 1960s and 1970s, when much plantation forest was cut down to fuel lime manufacture from the coral, it was probably already gone. (Even the birds "are not many anymore," an island-trekking brochure confesses, "since trees have been cutting down for human needs. We are all important in this universe, including birds.") According to the literature, the last Bali tiger vanished in the 1930s, but a few apparently persisted a few years longer, and rumors of tigers in the northwest mountains are still heard today. In July 1978, Dr. Seidensticker spoke with a local man who claimed to have observed a tiger one month earlier as it drank from a spring at the base of the great banyan that shaded his temple, and the following year a Bali newspaper printed reports that at least six tigers dwelled in Bali Barat, which was now a national park. I heard this, too, in 1996, and gazing at those mysterious high dark mountains, one longed to believe it. Pressed a little, however, my informants agreed that *harimau* had gone away for good.

In India, at simple rock shrines, one finds offerings to Vaghadeva, the tiger god, who is "guardian of the forest," as in Ussuria, and the goddess Durga rides upon a tiger bearing light and peace; she is the feminine power, or *sakti*, created by the gods to offset the aggressive male power that harms the world, and her image travels everywhere across India, blessing her realm from the sides of trucks and buses.

Having the same earth mother, man and tiger are perceived as brothers. In villages of the Warli tribe north of Bombay, wall paintings show the tiger ambling among men with a peaceful and benign demeanor. Tiger statues of carved wood, ubiquitous and sometimes phallic, are used in fertility rites to reflect the sexual endurance that has quickened the ancient trade in tiger nostrums; the phallic tiger may be decorated at harvest time with images of sun, moon, stars, and trees, and even entwined serpents. To propitiate Palaghata, goddess of marriage, bride and groom wear red-and-yellow shawls. If the goddess is pleased, the union is sanctified and the celebrants will be fertile; if not, the shawls turn into tigers, which devour them, for after all, one must never forget that the tiger is a tiger.

Though similar in aspect to *altaica*, the Indian or "Royal Bengal tiger," as it was known in the grand days of the Raj, shows less white on its flanks and underparts and in the calligraphic patterns of the head, and its flame color is more intense (*altaica* is less fire-orange

Crowning of the goddess Devi, Indian miniature, seventeenth century

than old gold). Also, it has more "double stripes" that split, then re-join at both ends. Called formerly *P. t. bengalensis*, it is now identified as *P. t. tigris*, the first-named or nominate race of the species tiger—arbitrarily, since the provenance of that first type specimen described by Linnaeus in 1758 (as *Felis tigris*) remains obscure. (I like to think it might have been a Caspian, since that race was closest to Europe geographically and also the first in 1815 to be given a subspecific name.) *P. t. tigris* ranged from the foothills of the Himalayas south throughout the Indian subcontinent, excepting Sri Lanka and the deserts of Gujarat and western Rajasthan, also northeastward across the borders in small numbers into western Myanmar and southern China. In recent years, it has been reported at elevations up to 13,000 feet in the mountains of Bhutan and also in southeastern Tibet, between the Tsangpo and Brahmaputra Rivers; one was tracked over Chimdor La Pass to the Tibetan Plateau at 15,000 feet, where no tiger had ever been reported. Since these wanderers kill domestic stock, it is supposed that they have been driven higher in their search for food as more and more lowland habitat becomes degraded.

For many centuries, Indian tigers were killed by the thousands to clear the country for mankind, but they were never seriously reduced until the advent of European firearms, which in combination with trained elephants made tiger-shooting one of the least sporting diversions ever devised. As more land was developed for tea plantations and firearms proliferated, the pace of tiger-killing markedly increased. By 1961, the hunter Jim Corbett (who traveled light and hunted man-eaters on foot and had already restricted himself to hunting that "large-hearted gentleman," as he once called it, with a cine-camera) was warning that the population had probably been reduced to some 2,000 animals. But even as late as 1965, some 400 tigers were still slaughtered annually, and within a few years, it became clear that the Bengal tiger—the emblematic monarch of zoo and circus that represents "tiger" to people the world over—was in severe decline throughout the subcontinent because of swollen human pressures from every side.

By the late 1960s, when researchers were estimating that no more than 600 tigers were left in all of Asia, a belated campaign to save this splendid creature got under way. In 1969, a first IUCN conference about the tiger crisis was held in New Delhi, and three years later, the IUCN, with WWF, initiated "Operation Tiger," designed to raise funds and public support for emergency tiger conservation programs in India and Southeast Asia. In response, India's President

Indira Gandhi sponsored an initiative called "Project Tiger," setting aside nine tiger reserves (the number has since grown to twenty-three) in which traditional activities, from hunting and gathering to grazing goats and cattle, were summarily banned, and human beings, too. In its first two decades, Project Tiger raised $30 million, a very large sum for conservation but insignificant in the face of the hard fact that ten new human beings for every dollar spent—300 million hungry mouths—were born in India in that same period.

Project Tiger was mainly funded by international nongovernmental organizations such as WWF, which put pressure on India's bureaucracy to produce immediate results. They got them, too, officially, at least, because bureaucrats from the smallest park official to the highest ministers reported nothing but the best possible news. By the mid-1980s, there seemed reason to believe that the Indian tiger population had more than doubled since 1972, to an estimated total of 4,300 animals, and that Project Tiger was one of the greatest triumphs in the history of wildlife conservation.

Of the tiger reserves, the most celebrated was Ranthambhore, in Rajasthan, a private province of the Maharajahs of Jaipur since the eighteenth century. (The deciduous dry upland forest at Ranthambhore is the westernmost range of *P. t. tigris*.) After Independence, in 1947, the incumbent maharajah had continued to use Ranthambhore as a preserve for hunting tigers, filling the blinds with august sportsmen such as Prince Philip of England, who was to become the honorary head of WWF. "*Bagh! Bagh!*" ("Tiger! Tiger!") cried the beaters, "moving the tiger toward the Prince," in the wry words of Fateh Singh Rahore, who worked in the preserve most of his life. (Possibly the Prince imagined that these bloody natives were imploring him to "bagh the tiger," which he did forthwith, no doubt from a seated position.)

Though the tiger had received official protection in 1959 (the same year the Chinese government was urging its eradication as a "pest"), it was not until 1970, after most of the tigers had been shot out, that these executions were actually put a stop to, and even six years after that, when a young man from Delhi, Valmik Thapar, made his first visit to Ranthambhore, the tigers were still scarce and rarely seen. Thapar spent three weeks driving up and down the dusty woodland roads before he set eyes on his first tiger, but in that sighting he recognized his life. Thapar became Fateh Singh's disciple, and a few years later they produced *With Tigers in the Wild*, the first of four popular books on tiger behavior.

In 1971, under the banner of Project Tiger, Fateh Singh as Ranthambhore's new game warden had "encouraged" the local villagers to move out of the park—not an inconsiderable task when one considers that even in the buffer zone surrounding the park boundaries, Ranthambhore had 200,000 poor farmers with 100,000 head of cattle. The only grazing left in this arid region was inside the park, and nine out of ten of the village families used wood from the park trees for cooking and keeping warm.

By 1979, the twelve poor villages in the center of the park had been relocated, forcibly where necessary. Two years later, Fateh Singh was badly beaten by the local men for his zealous insistence on park rules against hunting and gathering fodder, but the prey species were recovering in good numbers, and the tiger followed. Mr. Singh believes that at the time of his own compulsory relocation, in 1987, there were forty tigers in his small reserve, well protected, unafraid, and celebrated as the most readily observed and photographed in all of India.

When the impolitic Mr. Singh was removed from his post for zealous prosecution of his duties, Valmik Thapar, mistrusting the integrity and true intentions of the Park Service, established the Ranthambhore Foundation, which sought to work with local people toward finding ways to compensate them for their losses while lessening human impact on the park. But in this period, a fierce seven-year drought (and the absence of Fateh Singh's hard hand) encouraged the villagers to drive ever more herd animals inside the boundaries, causing further deterioration of the parched habitat. The loss of cover spread in the late eighties and early nineties, as drought and overgrazing continued, and meanwhile, the first signs were appearing that at Ranthambhore and elsewhere, too, the tigers were mysteriously disappearing.

Because tiger poaching at Ranthambore had been negligible before 1989, the sudden loss of tigers was at first blamed on the drought, but by the end of that year, it was all too clear that an organized slaughter was in progress. Under the noses of sixty forest guards, the missing animals had been shot and poisoned so rapidly and with such impunity that they were gone before the park authorities noticed, although the bitter villagers knew all about it.

In the winter of 1992, as a co-leader of an ornithological safari, I spent three days at Ranthambhore, a small, beautiful park set about with lotus lakes and ruins, including an immense and ancient Moghul fort that rises from cliff walls high above the forests. Chital deer, wild hog, and gazelle were everywhere, as if they, too, awaited the scarce tigers. Even the shy sambar deer were wandering out of the woodland, not because that was their habit nor because there were few tigers to disturb them, but because the understory in the deciduous dry forest around the lakes had been browsed clean by ravenous domestic stock, leaving no cover for wild animals on their way to water.

While at Ranthambhore, we paid a call on Fateh Singh, who has retained a kind of princely strut to go with his white mustache, safari clothes, and Stetson hat. As a kinsman of our colleague, the Delhi ornithologist Raj Singh, he gave us tea at his charming "farm" at the edge of the reserve, where poaching had increased so cruelly in the years since his retirement, he sighed, that it threatened to exterminate the tiger. Our chances of glimpsing *Bagh* these days were rather small, he warned.

Every day in the cold dawn, we passed through Ranthambhore's dark ancient portals to search the dirt roads and lake edges and dry grassy uplands for that gleam of fire. We enjoyed the fruit bats and large crocodiles and exotic birds—fish owls and painted snipe and crested serpent eagles and the lovely rose-ringed, Alexandrine, and blossom-headed parakeets, in a setting of ancient and overgrown temples and pavilions by the flowered lakeside. Perhaps it was this Arcadian realm that inspired tiger biologist Ullas Karanth to reflect, "When you see a tiger, it is always like a dream." Here and there we found fresh scrapes and pugmarks, but we saw no tiger.

Three months later, in May 1992, a large tiger-poaching operation was broken wide open at the nearby town of Sawai Madhopur, where we had boarded the Punjab Express to New Delhi. Most of the killing had been done by hunters of the Moghiya clan, using modern weapons—Gopal Moghiya claimed twelve tigers killed by his own group—but some was committed by village herdsmen who had sprinkled poison on fresh kills, knowing the tiger would return. Skins, bones, and organs were smuggled to Delhi's Sadar Bazaar for processing: the skins, which now brought $15,000 each, went mostly to the Arab countries, while the bones and parts, ground into powder, went to China, Taiwan, and Korea as well as large Asian colonies abroad. (Sadly, despite Buddhist proscriptions against taking life, the impoverished Tibetan refugee colony called Manju ka Tila, north of Delhi, as well as others at Dharmsala and Leh, had become heavily involved in all aspects of the tiger traffic, including the international network that smuggled the cargoes through such Himalayan towns as Simla and Srinigar and on across the high snow passes of Nepal and Tibet into East Asia.)

In the great furor that blew up around them, Project Tiger bureaucrats conceded that the tiger's recovery had been inflated in the first place in order to satisfy the Delhi politicians. An honest census was demanded, and when the smoke cleared, the park's estimated tiger population had been lowered from forty-five to twenty-eight. Even this figure was probably optimistic, all the more so since the poaching was still going on. According to Thapar, only fifteen tigers remained alive at Ranthambhore, including perhaps seven or eight that "do not show themselves."

In the few years of intensified poaching that began in 1988, about one-third of India's tigers had been destroyed, including an estimated 1,500 taken between 1990 and 1993—almost as many as were thought to survive in all of India when Project Tiger had commenced, twenty years before. India still claimed about half the world's tigers and was officially committed to protecting them, but almost nobody has faith in that commitment—or not, at least, in the present rancid atmosphere of governmental bribery and corruption. Except in a few well-guarded reserves, the Indian tiger was still hunted hard, even in the remote state of Assam, where guerrillas of the Boro tribe were trading tiger parts for armaments.

Akbar hunting a tiger near Gwalior, India, ca. 1590

The last great redoubt of *P. t. tigris* is the state of Madhya Pradesh, in the central highlands, which can claim more than half of India's remaining forests and arguably its highest density of tigers. The heart of the tiger country is a plateau in the Maikal range called Kanha, a region of mountainous ridges and ravines dominated by dry woodland and interspersed with savanna and maidans or meadows cleared in centuries past by the aboriginal Gond and Baiga cultivators. Here wildlife was still abundant as late as the early 1920s, when the region was reserved for gentlemanly tiger shoots by British notables. In the 1930s, Kanha was excluded from the hunting blocks and made a sanctuary, but after Independence, when much of the area was turned over to the local people to be cleared and tilled, it was opened up again for hunting. Between 1949 and 1951, a local maharajah shot thirty tigers in and around Kanha, causing general furor. By the time the sanctuary was reestablished, the remnant tigers were estimated at about nine animals.

In the mid-1960s, when George Schaller made a pioneering study of large Indian mammals, he chose Kanha as his research area, not only because it was large and remote—six or seven hours by bad road from the nearest provincial city—but because "there were more tigers at Kanha than in any other area that was visited." In the course of his work on the ungulates of the Kanha uplands, he would also make the first systematic observations on tiger ecology and behavior.

In 1974, Kanha became one of the first of the new reserves under Project Tiger, and two years later, substantially enlarged, it was made a national park. With 363 square miles altogether—not counting a larger buffer zone in which human activities would be restricted—it was now the largest park in all of India, although remote and little visited by foreigners. Because more than one hundred tigers were thought to live there, I went to Kanha in the winter of 1996. In eight glorious February days, I encountered all manner of exotic birds and beasts, including two Asian leopards, the enormous gaur, wild dog and blackbuck. The only large animal I failed to see was the Bengal tiger.

•   •   •

Another redoubt of the Indian tiger is the Sundarbans, on the Bay of Bengal in India and Bangladesh, where the great Ganges, Brahmaputra, and Meghna Rivers join to form a mangrove delta of 4,000 square miles, the largest on earth. Here tigers are exceptionally difficult to observe and study—so difficult that a recent writer made four trips, wrote a good book, and made a *National Geographic* film about Sundarbans tigers without ever setting eyes on even one.

In other days, tigers were common inland from the delta, but in the decade between 1930 and 1940, these fabled man-eaters were responsible for 186 recorded human deaths. In two campaigns (1927–41 and 1948–57), 424 tigers were destroyed, and by the early 1960s, the inland population had been extirpated and the few that wandered out of the labyrinth of mangrove islands were promptly shot. In the delta, however, the tiger continued to thrive, and it had not relinquished its man-eating habit; in the fishing villages, the people prayed to the goddess Bana Bibi to protect them. Electrified human dummies were set out to shock the tigers out of the idea of attacking upright figures, and food gatherers in the mangrove forest wore masks on the backs of their heads to deter tiger attacks (which almost invariably come from behind). It has been suggested that the saline habitat may be a factor in the man-eating habit, but John Seidensticker thinks it much more likely that the Sundarbans tigers are not accustomed to human company—as they are, for example, in more visited environments such as Ranthambhore, where at least a few tend to hang about the roads —and that their hunting instinct may be triggered by the solitary gatherers, who are frequently bent over in rough semblance of four-legged prey.

Though Bangladesh has now surpassed 100 million in population, the Sundarbans has been spared destruction by a century-long tradition of wise management. Unlike so many tiger range states with their conflicting authorities, Bangladesh placed the entire coastal region in the care of its excellent Forest Department, whose sustained-yield philosophy has increased food and fiber production without apparent damage to the system. Certain larger mammals have not survived—the rhino, hog deer, barasingha, and water buffalo—but these are primarily species of the drier delta, unsuited for life in brackish tidal swamp. On the other hand, the spotted deer (chital), wild boar, and tiger have done well, and the present estimate of 300 tigers in the Sundarbans seems reasonable to John Seidensticker, who found tracks of tigers and deer "throughout the forest." The mangrove wilderness, located in two countries, was assumed to be the largest contiguous tiger habitat on the subcontinent and one of the largest and most effective wildlife refuges in all South Asia, despite increasing pressure from the poachers. Indeed, few regions in the world, in Seidensticker's opinion, have ever matched its sheer biomass of ungulates—no doubt the main reason that this resilient animal adapted to a hostile saline habitat in the first place.

More recently, however, tiger biologist Ullas Karanth has been making an Indian tiger census using camera-traps, which are less fallible than pugmarks in identifying individual animals, and thus arriving at a more accurate count, and he has concluded—quietly, since he has no wish to confront his country's exceptionally touchy bureaucrats on this subject—that official estimates in recent years of tiger numbers and prey densities within the Sundarbans, which were never based on systematic assessment, are far too high. Also, the new

Geographic Information System (GIS) maps of the tiger range states show clearly that the Sundarbans is by no means the largest block of potential tiger habitat on the subcontinent, as had been thought. Even so, 4,000 square miles of mangrove delta, sensibly managed as a single unit for more than a century, would retain its critical long-term potential were it not for the new ambitions for the delta of the Asian Development Bank and other institutions more concerned with finance and development than with man's environment; today there is fear that the Sundarbans, long considered the last stronghold of *Panthera tigris*, may be doomed.

The southern forests and alluvial grasslands of the small states along the Himalayan front such as Nepal, Bhutan, and Assam are thought to be the finest tiger habitat in Asia; they include such celebrated reserves as Royal Chitwan in Nepal and Rajiji-Corbett, India's first national park, which was also first to be named a tiger sanctuary under Project Tiger in the early 1970s. In the same period, the Smithsonian-Nepal Tiger Ecology Project (the seed project for the present-day King Mahendra Trust for Nature Conservation) was established in Chitwan with John Seidensticker as a founding scientist. In the years since, this extended study has produced most of the little that is known about the dynamics of tiger populations. Subsequently, another long-term project was established by Ullas Karanth in southern India, at Nagarahole, and more recently, *tigris* research has been coordinated with fieldwork on the Amur, Indochinese, and Sumatran populations—all the extant tiger groups excepting the elusive tigers of South China, which may be extant or may not be.

Although a poor country, Nepal has provided considerable sums to protect and manage its 360-square-mile Royal Chitwan National Park in the Siwalik foothills, which supports the highest densities of tigers and tiger tourists in all Asia. A former hunting preserve, Chitwan is located in the Terai, a thousand-mile strip of forest and tall grassland under the south walls of the Himalayas. Rivaled only by the moist forests of the southwestern subcontinent (including Nagarahole) and perhaps Rajiji-Corbett Park across India's border to the east, Chitwan also gives sanctuary to leopard, Asian elephant, sloth bear, and the greater one-horned rhino. Chitwan adjoins Parsa Wildlife Reserve and India's Valmiki Tiger Reserve, which together comprise a vast border sanctuary that has since become a model for other parks.

Though not so dangerous as their kinsmen in the Sundarbans, the Chitwan tigers, about ninety strong, include a fair number of villagers in their diet—by unofficial estimate, about fifty since the park was founded in the early 1970s, or not quite two each year—and these killings occur despite the fact that prey is plentiful and the tigers are unprovoked. (In the past four centuries, tigers are thought to have killed 1,000,000 Asians, or about 2,500 people annually, or twenty-five people per 1,000 tigers—not an unreasonable figure when one considers that a man-eater of yore would often kill that many and more all by itself. In this past century, of course, human mortalities have declined for want of tigers, despite the increase in density of this form of prey.)

Leopards, like dholes (wild dogs) and wolves, are said to be scarce where tigers prosper, but in Chitwan and Kanha, where prey is abundant, these large predators seem more tolerant of one another. Also, the assumption that tigers are solitary has been questioned by Valmik Thapar. "I think tigers were forced into solitary and nocturnal lives as a result of persecution and habitat destruction, leading to shortage of prey," Thapar has said. "In effectively protected habitats, such as Ranthambhore during the 1980s, tigers may form temporary groups in order to hunt, and may even share food, as lions do." On the other hand, these tiger groups—usually a female with young, some-times fitfully attended by a male—lack the stability that is seen in lion clans.

Dr. Alan Rabinowitz of WCS has recently discovered to his own surprise that in "classic tiger parks" such as Alaungdaw Kathapa National Park in Myanmar, even where ungulates are relatively abundant, the leopard and wild dog may be common but the tiger is far less common than was thought. "Nobody went out into the field and had a good look for themselves, and even when they did, they were so inexperienced that they saw leopard tracks and called them tiger." I asked him if, as tiger biologists agree, prey density was the critical factor in tiger conservation, then what was the significance of tiger absence where the prey population is so dense?

"Seidensticker's work has shown that tigers tend to drive out leopards under normal conditions," he said, "but the leopard can sub-sist on much smaller prey and also in more marginal conditions, and the wild dog is a far more efficient hunter, with a much higher per-centage of successful kills; also, when large ungulates are scarce, the dogs can always split the pack and hunt down smaller prey. In other words, we can lock up that park, protect the habitat and the prey pop-ulations, and still fail to restore the tiger. I can only speculate that where tiger numbers have been seriously reduced by human activities, including poaching, the tiger may have difficulty recovering its niche."

Belinda Wright, an attractive and spirited tiger partisan and filmmaker whose wonderful *Land of the Tiger*, shot at Kanha and Ranthambhore, is the best film on its photogenic subject I have ever seen, was kind enough to put me up in her small house on the outskirts of Delhi. For three days and evenings, we discussed the tiger and its future and also the painful subject of the tribal people whose villages lie within the Kanha boundaries. These people are being relocated against their will to marginal and degraded land outside their forests—the common fate of "tribals" or "traditionals" ever since the concept of wildlife reserves and parks was introduced by colonial administrators into Asia and Africa. Perhaps because she was born in India and loves its remote regions, Wright does not share the caste indifference to the welfare of her country's indigenous people. These days, in fact, she was demanding better treatment for the small, dark hunter-gatherers who were being shunted out of Kanha. For decades, "keeping people separate from animals" has been the conventional wisdom among wildlife conservationists, although forest peoples everywhere, having no choice about it, have lived in respectful balance with their habitat for millennia and, like the immortal Dersu, are careful to allow the tiger to go its way in peace. Surely they disturb the forest less than the noise and pollution of trucks, roads, buildings, comfortable accommodations, plumbing, and the proliferating apparatus of tiger tourism or even field research.

In 1973, when Project Tiger was getting started, many tiger reserves were summarily emptied of their human inhabitants—about 4,000 villagers in Chitwan alone (although the removal of these people had actually begun back in the 1960s, to protect not the tiger but the King's hunting preserve and the vanishing one-horned rhino). But in Chitwan, unlike Ranthambhore, the 300,000 local people in the buffer zones were at least permitted to enter the park to collect thatch for their houses, and today from one third to one half of all entrance fees in this most popular of Asian wildlife parks is set aside for schools and clinics and other benefits to the community. Also, its people are given work in park concessions—elephant rides, nature walks, a hostel with tiger lookouts, and the like. It may or may not be coincidence that the poaching crisis at Chitwan has abated, with the tigers and the endangered rhinos doing fine.

Similarly, at Nagarahole, relocation of villagers had been urged by Western conservation groups, including WCS, which sponsors Ullas Karanth's long-term research. Despite the promise of community improvement in the form of new schools and clinics, there was, inevitably, resentment. One published report quoted a visiting WCS administrator as saying that "relocating tribal or traditional people who live in these protected areas is the single most important step toward conservation" and also that the people's food-hunting in the park was "compulsive." Though this report turned out to be problematical, relocation remains a painful issue, and Karanth himself has expressed regret that the resettlement of a thousand "squatters" from Nagarahole between 1970 and 1980 "was not handled with the required degree of compassion, sensitivity, and planning."

More recently, reports appeared in *The Guardian* and elsewhere about WCS, Smithsonian, and Save the Tiger Fund endorsement of a vast new wildlife park being established in Myanmar by an unsavory military dictatorship known as the State Law and Order Restoration Committee (SLORC), which was said to be clearing out the region with brutal expulsions of the traditional Karen people. At a WCS dinner in New York City, I asked George Schaller whether dealing with a repressive regime and thereby giving it legitimacy might not harm future conservation efforts in the Third World. Frowning, Schaller made the point that conservation organizations and their biologists cannot concern themselves with the politics and short-term activities of Third World governments, which tend to come and go, but must focus instead on long-term objectives on behalf of imperiled wildlife, biodiversity, and natural habitat, which are disappearing and irreplaceable. Ullas Karanth, who had joined our conversation, seemed to agree.

I had heard this reasoning before, of course, not only from George but from other conservation biologists, and it sounded eminently sensible each time I heard it. And as it happened, the Myanmar reports turned out to be exaggerated and inflammatory, too—further evidence of how very carefully foreign groups must tread in situations involving wildlife and local people. But such reports pointed also to an underlying hazard with which field biologists and their organizations are faced increasingly in Third World countries—those cases involving implicit institutional acceptance of an uneasy triage in which resources are gambled on a future for rare creatures rather than on easing the lot of wretched and defenseless members of our own species.

Since talking with Schaller, I have discussed this thorny issue with Drs. Karanth and Rabinowitz, Hornocker and Quigley, Seidensticker and Miquelle. Though he seemed as troubled by the dilemma as the others, Dale was vehement and clear in defense of relocation. "After all," he argued, "with widespread destruction of habitat, over-exploitation of resources, and loss of biodiversity, Asian tribal people can no longer be said to be living in balance with their environment. Therefore, efforts to maintain islands of habitat in the sea of humanity in Asia are not unreasonable. Preservation of natural conditions, clean water, flood and erosion control, and the resources these can provide are critical to the life quality of local people, too. Our great failure has been, not indifference to the poor, but our ongoing refusal to address the human overpopulation problem. Ultimately the survival of our species must depend on finding a balance between human numbers and a sustainable use of resources."

For our common future, we had to ensure as best we could the integrity of our habitat and the great shimmering web of biodiversity that includes the tiger. To achieve that, in the short term, disagreeable and undemocratic measures have become necessary in certain localities where our human numbers are overwhelming land and life. (Unless we come to our senses about world resource limits a lot faster than the corporation-owned world governments are doing at present, these will not be the last such drastic measures, not by any means.) But in the long term, such methods will be useless unless the proliferating poor are taken care of, too. It is not "they" who are too many; it is "we" as a species who are too many. To drive them from their home territories because they are in the way, therefore expendable (one thinks uneasily about Mao's attitude toward wildlife), is another sign of what world competition for the earth's diminishing resources has already come to.

What seems unjust is that the penalty for saving tigers—as we must—falls entirely upon the rural poor, who must live with them for better or worse, with all of the drawbacks and the dangers and few or none of the rewards. Surely compensation must be found for that real sacrifice, if only to avoid revenge against the tiger. With the pitiless increase in human populations, the millions of landless people at the edge of famine will inevitably turn away from the wild animals of their ancient myths and animist religions; increasingly they must resent the investment of unimaginable resources on behalf of wild creatures from whose protection they derive no benefit and which represent, on the contrary, a present danger to their families and domestic stock. Seeking to console themselves for what has been taken from them—unjustly, as they see it—they will cling to the tree-cutting, hunting, and gathering which was never illegal before the advent of the park but, rather, an aspect of their daily life.

Since the self-fulfilling murder of Dian Fossey, who perceived the local African as the natural enemy of the mountain gorilla, therefore herself, conservation biologists and environmentalists have become increasingly open to the participation of local villagers in decisions affecting their own welfare—an unheard-of indulgence when viewed from the colonial perspective, yet a welcome change from that Raj-influenced elitism that still constipated certain wildlife organizations when Project Tiger was first established.

Because of her active investigations of the tiger trade, Belinda Wright's work is dangerous; her house and garden are enclosed by a steel fence, with heavy locks and two permanent guards. Also, our conversations were regularly interrupted by cryptic phone calls from her network of informers. One man, a jeweler, had just been offered two poached skins and might cooperate in setting up a "sting"; another came by later in the morning, not wishing to risk a tap on Belinda's phone.

One evening we went to dinner at the house of Valmik Thapar, a huge bearded man with an intense, brooding demeanor—not in the least like the warm and cozy Thapar in Sikh turban who would subsequently appear on world television as host of an excellent series on Indian wildlife. Also present was their friend Bittu Sahgal, the impassioned editor of *Wild Asia*. When I asked Thapar how much Fateh Singh had known about the extent of local poaching when he spoke with us at Ranthambhore four years earlier, "Valu" Thapar confessed that Fateh Singh had alerted him about the crisis as early as 1991, but "I discounted it. I did not want to believe what was happening to our tigers."

Despite all Thapar's efforts at local education, Ranthambhore had been hammered hard since Fateh Singh's departure, with herders and woodcutters—and poachers, too—infesting the whole park. He doubted that any of the smaller parks could support a tiger population very much longer. True, the poaching seemed to have died down a little, but the tiger reserve system in India was "in tatters" due to agricultural encroachment and livestock grazing.

Faced with government indifference to the epidemic poaching and the utter ineffectuality of WWF-India, which was controlled by socialites, Valu and Belinda, with Ullas Karanth and Bittu Sahgal, had founded the Wildlife Protection Society of India (WPSI), whose foremost mission is the arrest and prosecution not only of poachers but of the animal-parts traders who encouraged the poaching and made most of the money. Recently, this small and intense group had been joined by Ashok Kumar of WWF-International's TRAFFIC department, which concerns itself with the animal-parts trade the world over. ("What will it say about the human race if we let the tiger go extinct?" Kumar has asked, in a *Time* story with the cover line "DOOMED." Kumar and Wright are in agreement that local people must be encouraged to take part in wildlife conservation, and "can be recruited to contribute significantly toward . . . habitat protection if they are involved in forest management and accorded a share of the benefits.")

Mostly because of Belinda Wright's undercover operations, eighty-two people had been taken to court for wildlife violations, but every last one had been set free. Though not embittered like Thapar and Sahgal, Wright wondered if India had the will to save its wildlife, since the massive corruption in high places that was being exposed in daily scandals while I was in Delhi had further weakened the puny resolve Project Tiger had once inspired in politicians. Nevertheless, these WPSI activists, despite frequent and spirited disputes, are closely bonded in their strong commitment. They have no idea what effect their group will have on India's bureaucracy, yet believe they are witnessing small signs of progress. Whatever happens, Wright and Thapar say their lives are dedicated to the fight to save the tiger, which is, as Bittu Sahgal says, "the soul of India."

At our first meeting a few years ago, John Seidensticker was courteous enough to appear interested in my queries about the phylogeny of *P. tigris*. He was also sympathetic with my uneducated doubts about what seemed an arbitrary splitting of the species into eight subspecies or races, when in all likelihood, the mainland tigers—the Caspian may have been the lone exception— were a single unbroken population before the advent of man and agriculture and the ensuing fragmentation of their Asian range. Without criticizing the taxonomists, John suggested persuasively that "ecotype" might be a more useful designation than subspecies or geographic race for a creature which seems equally well adapted to temperate woodlands and tropical rain forest, marine mangrove forest and long-grass Himalayan foothills, riverine thicket and the vast reed beds of western Asia's inland seas; alternatively, one might speak of tiger "bio-regions" such as Ussuria, the Indian sub-continent, Southeast Asia, and the islands, in which morphological changes had become established in regional populations. Tiger morphology, after all, reflected the animal's habitat rather than its geographic range. Thus, the pelage of the smaller, darker tigers of the south might be a hunting adaptation to the deep jungle shadows of the tropics.

According to a recent analysis by scientists of the National Cancer Institute, a genetic molecular assessment of the tigers reveals a "relatively low level of genetic variation among all tiger subspecies." Dr. Stephen O'Brien and his colleagues have concluded that "a recent homogenization of the entire species (before their radiation into distinct geographic populations), and an even more recent geographic isolation of no longer than 10,000 years ago, has been insufficient time for subspecies-level genetic adaptations to become apparent." This assessment supports Kitchener's morphological review of tiger pelages and skeletal remains, and it tends to bear out Seidensticker's suggestion that the identification of tiger subspecies is essentially invalid and that trinomials such as *altaica* are mainly useful as a means of referring to geographic populations.

In recent GIS maps, some 160 separate tiger habitats have been identified, most of them fragmented into many smaller units; all of these have become isolated from one another by impassable barriers of hostile territory due to the activities of man. Of the 160 habitats, perhaps twenty-five at most are large enough, with sufficient prey, to remain viable into the new millennium, always assuming man's protective care. But even if all necessary steps to protect the last wild tigers are undertaken, that may not be enough. Conservation biologists have learned through hard experience that for large felids, including tigers, traditional conservation management techniques have failed or are failing throughout Asia. In a recent paper, Dr. Seidensticker discusses the lack of significant progress even where protection has been increased, and points out unmistakable indications that about half the world's endangered mammals are already beyond the reach of increased protective efforts alone: effective restoration now demands corrective and preventive measures to make sure that benign neglect (as in Java and Bali, where the tiger went extinct despite a system of protected reserves with suitable habitat) does not permit some imbalance to occur that proves fatal to the tiger before that threat is properly understood.

One April day in 1996, John Seidensticker was kind enough to give Belinda Wright and me a close look at his two Sumatran tigers, in their private cages behind the exhibit pens at the

National Zoo. Through the bars from just a yard away, we peered into the strange agate eyes of a full-grown young male, baring its teeth in a low, growling snarl. It was a small tiger, perhaps two and a half feet at the shoulder, which is little more than half the height of a male *altaica*. (A typical female might weigh 160 pounds, or approximately the weight of a male cougar.) Curiously, the diameter of its paw is relatively larger than in other tigers, and recalling that wolves have large, broad pads for travel on the snow, I wondered aloud about a "snowshoe" adaptation for muddy and slippery tropical terrain. Seidensticker only grunted in response to this brilliant theory.

The skull and face of the *sumatrae* race are narrower than in larger tigers, and it seems to have a more pronounced white ruff. The pelage is dark red in tone, and its flanks appear more heavily striped farther down around the belly, which is a dingy, sallow white by comparison with the bright white of *altaica* and *tigris*. Its stripes (which may be spotted at the tips) are more numerous and closely set, and the white pattern of its visage is much reduced by comparison to the bold harlequin faces of the larger tigers. All these characters contribute to the rather dark, cryptic appearance of this island race. (In a black-and-white photograph taken years ago at the Berlin Zoo, two Javan tigers appear even darker and more closely striped than these Sumatrans, and the Bali form is said to have been darkest of all.)

(In my notes that day, I recorded a vague impression that apart from its darker pelage and small size, this animal looked oddly "different" from the larger tigers, and so I was mildly gratified by an article that appeared in the September 1998 issue of the British journal *Animal Conservation*. Close analysis of its DNA, its author said, revealed that *sumatrae* is genetically distinct from other tigers, which

Sumatran tiger (P. t. sumatrae)

suggests it diverged from the mainland form earlier in the course of tiger evolution than had been thought. Presumably, the extinct *sondaica* and *balica*, to which *sumatrae* would seem to be sibling if not ancestral, were also populations of this separate race.)

In the new millennium, *Panthera tigris*, in its remnant groups, walks the edge of the great abyss of extinction. The Bali, Caspian, and Javan populations are already gone, and the South China, Sumatran, and Amur races, which can claim scarcely 1,000 animals among them, may vanish forever in the first decades of the new century. As for the others, the latest estimate for the Indochinese tiger is 1,500, and for the Indian or Bengal race perhaps 3,000. *P. t. tigris* can still claim over half of all the wild tigers left on earth, and almost ten times the number of Amur tigers. Thus it would appear that because of its broad range and distribution, which includes such strongholds as Chitwan, Corbett, Manas (in Bhutan), Nagarahole, and the Sundarbans, *P. t. tigris* is the tiger with the best chance of survival in the next millennium, and most authorities continue to assume that the main hope for the species lies with this race.

On the other hand, one cannot speak of "3,000 Indian tigers" when that population has been scattered into well over one hundred isolated units, with all but a few of these strung out in unsustainable small bands of stressed tigers restricted to small pockets of a sadly tattered habitat surrounded by hordes of food-and-fuel-seeking human beings and their famished herds. These isolated groups, in many cases too inbred to maintain a vital population, are dying out ever more rapidly. In certain reserves the tigers are doing well, but as a race, *tigris* continues to diminish. If the tigers of the subcontinent could be reunited in a single population in a single region—which is the great hope in the Sikhote-Alin—the future of the Indian tiger would seem far more hopeful.

In 1992, when I first visited the Russian Far East, it was widely believed that the Amur tiger might be extinct as early as the year 2000. But *altaica* has its own signal advantages, every one of them corollary to the fact that it is essentially a single population in a single habitat that is more or less continuous throughout its range. No other tiger population inhabits a vast and almost roadless area of forested mountains, very thinly populated by human beings. Also, despite its dangerously low numbers, *altaica* is slowly increasing, while *tigris*, beset by *Homo sapiens*, continues its remorseless slow decline.

The Siberian Tiger Project scientists have always believed that in the end, *altaica* has the best chance of any of the tigers, and to my astonishment John Seidensticker agrees ("Don't tell my friends in In-

dia," he says ruefully). This is partly due to his admiration for the work of the Siberian Tiger Project scientists, in particular the recent papers published by Dale Miquelle and Evgeny Smirnov; he believes that such hope as exists for the Amur race depends on these exceptionally able and committed researchers, and perhaps especially upon Miquelle, "a very smart, thoughtful, complex, 'tough' man who I believe has been looking for [his] home and found it with tigers and the Russian Far East."

"When I first went to Terney, the smells and the sights triggered in my mind very early childhood memories from Butte and Twin Bridges, Montana, where I grew up. And what a country! Visiting the Russian Far East was like going back in time to the Montana my grandfather talked about." Seidensticker, very stirred, believed that a similar "recognition of place" had seized the imaginations of Maurice Hornocker and the other American researchers. "The Russian Far East is a powerful, big, wild country . . . this was Yellowstone and Montana and Idaho all together, nearly a century earlier."

In January 1996, I found my chance to accept Maurice Hornocker's kind invitation to return to Ussuri Land in winter, when tracking a tiger, and even sighting one, might be possible. In the low sun of winter, the silver aircraft from Alaska crossed the bright volcanoes of Kamchatka and descended into the Siberian barrens at an airport of big urine-colored buildings some fifty miles inland from the gold-mining settlement at Magadan. There snow was falling on deep snow, and the temperature was −48°F.

Continuing south over the Okhotsk Sea, the plane crossed endless distances of pack ice split by jagged black crevasses that zigzagged away into the mists like frozen lightning—an icescape of doomsday and hallucination, rigid and empty. The stewardess's instructions in

the event of a forced landing seemed quite pointless, since at such deadly temperatures, with help so far away, nothing would avail any survivors. Below the wing, a surf of ice had fetched up on a black-rock peninsula that jutted westward from dark snow-striped mountains—the north point of Sakhalin Island, where Anton Chekhov once served as a doctor and where the Exxon Corporation and other multinationals are said to be "developing" the oil. Not until the plane had crossed the endless frozen delta of the Amur River did the ice tumult give way to snowbound tundra and spruce muskeg. Five hundred miles upriver, it set down briefly at Khabarovsk before flying south over Ussuria to Vladivostok.

All day the plane had kept up with the sun, which remained low in the south, but as it rose from Khabarovsk and turned up the ice-locked Ussuri, the sun set at last over Manchuria, and the deep blue of the wild horizon was fired by a dragon light of crimson. To the east, where night had fallen over the Japan Sea, Orion rode on a clear void of black sky.

At Vladivostok airport I was met by Howard Quigley and Dale Miquelle, who was now field director of the Siberian Tiger Project, based in this old port city. On the long drive to town, we stopped for supper at the "Vlad Motor Inn," created and shipped piece by piece from Canada in an effort to re-create an "American" atmosphere where Western businessmen might feel at home. As we departed, the receptionist said, "Okay. Good night. All my best."

In southeastern Siberia in the depths of winter, it is dark until 8 a.m. The window of my chilly room at the Hotel

Vladivostok (where bear gallbladders, it was said, might be purchased in the lobby at $10 a gram) had a fine prospect of the great white Amur Bay; at daylight, hunched figures like black ciphers were already transfixed on the frozen waste. Fueled by hot coffee, I walked out onto the ice to investigate their catch, a small herring or smelt known as *korushka*. For sheer hardihood, these fishers' only rivals are the waterfront mongers, who peddle king crab, rock-hard fishes such as humpback salmon, carp, herring, whiting, and a kind of cod, along with a few specimens of the giant greenish trout known as the *taimen*. The fishmongers work in an icy wind off the frozen bay, where the only birds are the hard-bitten scavengers—the glaucous, herring, and black-tailed gulls and the sea eagles.

An hour later, sky and ice turn blue, and drab colors emerge from the clothing of the stumpy fishers. A magpie flapped and sailed among the dark Mongolian oaks along the waterfront, where a large bronze statue of a tiger guards the seawalls. In the frozen winter of 1986, four tigers visited the city. The last of these was a 440-pound male which appeared in March and caught and ate a dog. Despite the tiger's place of honor on the city crest, this marauding specimen was destroyed at a trolley station from a helicopter. In the neighborhood of the bronze tiger, on a street leading from the bay, was the Arseniev Museum, named for the explorer, where the ancient natural history collection, with its yellow-pale, dusty, and tattered tiger, lynx, and Amur leopard, might well have been assembled back in Dersu's day.

From the museum, Dr. Quigley and I continued downhill in this small city—at present, a half-million people—to the Avenue 25th October (an anachronism even in Vladivostok, where Leninski Prospekt had already been changed back to Svetlanski). On the main square was Primorski Krai's vast "White House" administration building, built by the Soviets, and also some small open-air markets that sold dinky frozen fish and chicken limbs, pine nuts, garlic, wizened apples, candies, cigarettes, and the dog-eared dolls and weary souvenirs of seaside summers. Not far away was the yellow terminal of the trans-Siberian railway, which goes north to the Amur at Khabarovsk, then due west to Lake Baikal and Moscow on its journey of 6,000 miles and seven time zones. We walked a footbridge over the tracks and descended to the waterfront, where a retired Soviet submarine was on display. A pair of white-tailed eagles flew the icy skies, crossing the peaks of the black and bony masts of an old sailing ship that might have been docked there since the days of Vitus Bering.

Dale Miquelle joined us for supper at the Restaurant Okeon, which like so many local businesses and apartment buildings was soiled and depressing on the outside but more or less comfortable within. Located on the waterfront down the hill from the bronze tiger, "The Ocean" served such delicacies as Fat Pullet Breast Plump and Chiken Lag with Mashrooms. Dale's Russian, exuberant as ever, had much improved since my first visit more than three years earlier, and he would serve as our interpreter throughout the visit.

My companions brought me up to date on the progress of the Siberian Tiger Project, which had already acquired a far more precise understanding of tiger predation and predation rates and also a better understanding of home range size for both male and female tigers in Ussuria; these data were crucial in determining the area required for effective protection and for future planning. Much had also been learned about reproduction—birthrates, intervals between litters, cub survival rates—the better to assess the long-term impact of chronic poaching and the resilience and viability of this population. With the first longitudinal studies of individual tigers made possible by radio telemetry, the project was gaining critical information about social habits—how often tiger pairs associated as well as mated, or how many litters a tigress might produce within a lifetime. In these first years of the project, a dozen litters that had produced almost thirty new tigers had been documented. Yet many questions were still unanswered. For example, a recent increase in tiger numbers had not been accompanied by a decrease in their prey, suggesting that despite local rumor to the contrary, they were not really competing with the local hunters for game.

Thirteen of the thirty-odd tigers using the Sikhote-Alin Reserve had been captured and fitted with radio collars and returned to the wild without a casualty. Of this group, two had been lost to natural causes: one had been crushed by a falling limb, another had wandered out of radio contact. Two others had not been located since early 1995 and had probably been killed by poachers, although a project tiger had been reported about one hundred miles to the south, near the mining settlement at Dalnegorsk. At present, nine "marked" animals were being monitored.

The tiger decline that inspired the Save the Tiger campaigns of the early 1970s had mainly been caused by loss of habitat, including prey, and by overhunting, not only for sport but for the high market value of the skins. Only in China, in the 1950s, had the tiger been bountied and slaughtered as a "pest." Those dead tigers had become state property, and a considerable stockpile of tiger bones used in traditional medicines had been accumulated.

For perhaps as long as 4,000 years, the trade in tiger medicines—
pulverized tiger bone (the front leg bone, the humerus, is considered
the most efficacious); also, such folk remedies as tiger-eye pills, tiger-
bone wine, tiger-brain lotion, tiger tail, and tiger-penis soup—had
been respectable as well as profitable. (Outside Asia, "tiger-bone
medicine" has been too easily dismissed as superstitious hocus-pocus
in the same category as rhino horn, when, in fact, its anti-
inflammatory effect in arthritis and other ailments has been asserted
if not confirmed by some pharmacological researchers in Western
laboratories.)

China had always been the chief instigator of the tiger trade and
chief consumer, and as its tigers disappeared, it sought to develop new
sources of supply. In 1986, the Hengdaohezi Tiger Breeding Center
was established in Heilongjiang Province for the declared purpose of

butchering and selling those animals which succumbed to "natural causes or disease." The tiger farm was condemned by environmental groups, which feared it would encourage tiger-parts traffic and serve as a shelter and market for the poaching trade, which had suddenly started to proliferate even as tigers everywhere were disappearing.

The depletion of China's hoard of tiger bones partly explains the upsurge of the trade in the late 1980s, when poaching intensified in India, Bhutan, Indochina, Indonesia, and the Russian Far East. Many of the beautiful golden hides eventually made their way to the Arab states, while the bones went to dealers in China and Hong Kong, Taiwan and Korea, Singapore, Japan, and the large Asian communities abroad.

In Russia, most of the blame was laid on the Chinese, who were willing to pay a middleman up to $10,000 for a single tiger—more than an ordinary Russian might make in five years' work. The poachers were hungry for the prices paid in China, not only for the beautiful striped pelt of Hu Lin, the King, but for those "medicine bones" ground down to powder and consumed not only for their healthful properties but in the hope of acquiring the tiger's strength, particularly its legendary potency, which permits it to mate vigorously several times each hour throughout a period of several days. Tonics and potions brewed from genitalia were much in favor among rich, flagging Asians, and a dried penis (which resembles a coiled eel) could command up to $2,500 in Singapore or Taiwan, where bowls of nice hot penis soup, $300 each, were consumed for their restorative properties in man's struggle against such dire afflictions as impotence and death. (In Hong Kong, a delightful bogus penis ingeniously fashioned of animal sinew could be snapped up by the discriminating shopper for $15.)

In South Korea, tiger bones were sought avidly by dealers in traditional medicines, or *hamyak*. Musk-deer glands and bear gallbladders sold briskly, too.

As early as 1975, CITES had banned international trade in all tigers and their parts except the Amur tiger. Yet between 1975 and 1992, South Korea alone imported 13,510 pounds of tiger bone, with an annual average of 750 pounds (one tiger provides thirteen to twenty-four pounds of powdered bone); from 1988 to 1992 came a sharp increase to 1,272 pounds annually. (In the same period, this small nation imported between fifty-two and ninety-six dead tigers every year.) Before 1992, most of the imports had come from Indonesia, with China a poor second; in that year, China, buying from thriving poaching rings all over eastern Asia, became the foremost exporter of dried bones. In the next few years, the street value of a single tiger rose as high as $25,000, with an estimated sixty animals poached annually from 1990 to 1994. (At about $50 per gram [the price paid in Japan], a large frozen male tiger from Primorski Krai which brought the hunter perhaps $8,000 might fetch an eventual street price of $750,000 for its 15 kilograms of powdered bones.)

By September 1993, CITES had warned Taiwan, China, South Korea, and Hong Kong against this trade and threatened sanctions. Subsequently, these countries were cleared by a CITES report about their "progress," despite convincing evidence that China had exported 1.5 tons of tiger bone—more than 200 tigers—to South Korea between June and September of that year alone. The following March, officials of twelve tiger range states—all but China, which boycotted the meeting—met in Delhi to exchange information and methods of tiger protection for the future; and the following month, the United States, unwilling to displease China, levied trade sanctions against Taiwan for trafficking in products from endangered species, especially the tiger and black rhino—the first trade sanctions the United States had ever issued in the name of wildlife protection.

In 1993, China banned internal trade in tiger bone, at least officially, and the other Asian countries went along. Only North Korea and Japan (which also remains obdurate in its intention to continue the slaughter of whales for "research" purposes) refused to close their markets. By 1995, tiger-bone products were no longer sold openly in Asian markets, which actually declined. However, a covert trade continued, and it was assumed that China was still behind it.

With the collapse of the Soviet Union, improvised local poaching in the Russian Far East had made way for a criminal enterprise rumored to have been taken over by the mafia, and for a time, it appeared to be the most virulent in Asia. In 1993, Russian authorities and American environmentalists led by Global Survival Network, with funding for fifteen rangers and sufficient vehicles and equipment to cover the whole range of *altaica*, set up a mobile anti-poaching unit called Operation Amba, which went into the field in the winter of 1994. (Most organized poaching takes place in the winter, when tigers are easily tracked.) Using local informants, surprise tactics, rumor, and the media, striking and disappearing like guerrillas, Amba rangers under the command of a Ministry of the Environment official named Vladimir Shetinin were able to persuade the poachers and traders that their operation was far more pervasive than it was. Finally, in August 1995, when tiger protection received the support of Prime Minister Victor Chernomyrdin in a national decree, local law enforcement officials and the judiciary began to respond more seriously to the crisis.

Operation Amba had learned quickly to hire, train, and work with local people, to equip them properly, and to pay them on time, a most unusual accommodation in the new Russia. Using local support to catch the lawbreakers and legal support to punish them, Amba and other ranger groups (the internationally sponsored patrols that protect the zapovedniks) crippled organized poaching. By 1996, when I returned to Siberia, the tigers had started to come back. The next year, only eleven would be poached, and the numbers continue to shrink, partly because of a drastic reversal in the consumer economies of "the Asian tigers." With fewer buyers and a smaller payoff, poachers and traders saw no sense in risking jail.

Meanwhile, Chinese medicine manufacturers, joining environmentalists at an international conference in Hong Kong in 1998, had agreed to seek substitutes for tiger medicines to help reduce the traffic in rare creatures. After the conference, China officially outlawed all sales of tiger parts. Today there is an expanded trade in non-tiger-bone nostrums derived from domestic animals, also leopard, bear, and mole-rat, or zokor (mole-rat wine, known as *sai-long*, is apparently very popular), yet China is said to be stockpiling bone against the day when the tiger traffic might resume. As for the Hengdaohezi Tiger Breeding Center in Heilongjiang, which for a time was the main source of bones for an illegal tiger-wine manufacturer, it has become the "Siberia Tiger Park," relying for support on busloads of Chinese tourists who come across the Sungari River from Harbin to watch the live tigers in the enclosures capture and eat chickens.

In cold clear weather, in the early morning, we picked up Anatoli Astafiev, director of the Sikhote-Alin Reserve, whom I had seen last at the zapovednik meeting held at Bolshe Khetskhir in the early summer of 1992. At the airport we boarded a flight to the airstrip at Plastun, not far south of Terney. The small plane crossed broad white potato fields and rice paddies on its way to the south end of the mountains, then followed the east slope of the Sikhote-Alin north along the coast.

These tumultuous small mountains of the Russian Far East are all but uninhabited, but logging tracks meander like deer trails across the ridges and high plateaus, and skid tracks for felled trees scar the mountainsides like claw swipes. The logging and mining of Siberia are inevitable in this time of economic desperation, and the last un-logged river basins in Primorski Krai are the Bikin and the Samaga in the north. Tiger and elk cannot adapt to the clear-cut forestry favored by American lumber corporations, and although they do better in areas of selective cutting, this method unfortunately requires a far greater extent of forest and a mesh of logging roads, which erode the mountainsides and muddy the rivers and open the wilderness to the vehicles and guns of professional poachers as well as to opportunistic hunters, often the drivers of the logging trucks.

The tiger is an exceptionally resilient animal, adapting to a range of habitats perhaps unmatched by any other large mammal except man. It can even subsist in the neighborhood of man's activities (where man permits this or cannot prevent it), which supports the idea that the habitat itself is of secondary significance so long as it provides the tiger with enough to eat. Increasingly, the maintenance of prey density has been recognized as the most important element in habitat protection, and field biologists working with rare animals have realized that they can no longer limit themselves to pure research in the field but must also work as conservationists in wildlife

management, lest their study species disappear before their eyes. In recent years, in fact, field researchers have adopted the name "conservation biologists." And "that's all right," Maurice Hornocker cautions, "but you have to start with the biology."

Siberian Tiger Project research had already made clear that its sparse prey base was a far more serious threat to the Amur tiger than destruction of habitat or even moderate poaching. Ungulates both large and small are far more abundant in Southeast Asia and the Indian subcontinent than in these northern woodlands: in 500 square miles of deciduous forest and long grass in Nepal, for example, fifty tigers might find plenty to eat, whereas in the taiga, where the game animals are scarce and scattered, a territory of the same size might support only four or five tigers, and even these would be obliged to hunt much harder, especially the females tending cubs.

Altaica's total remaining range in the Russian Far East, from Khabarovski Krai south through Primorski Krai to the North Korea border, was approximately 60,000 square miles, about 7 percent of which had been set aside in zapovedniki. While most were located in Primorski Krai, a 1996 survey would report that forty-eight to fifty-three adult tigers—about 14 percent of the whole population—still wandered Khabarovski Krai, as far north as the northern limit of the elk and boar. Throughout this region, the majority lived outside the reserves, but in the winter of 1995, the prey animals were four to ten times more abundant in the reserves than outside it, and therefore the tigers were more abundant, too. The populations of wild game, hunted relentlessly since state supervision of firearms was eased in the mid-eighties, were now so low that the habitat outside the reserves might well have reached its carrying capacity for tigers. (Tiger density over the Amur's entire present range has been estimated at one per 190 square miles, versus four within the Sikhote-Alin Reserve and thirty-two in Chitwan, in Nepal.)

The Sikhote-Alin Reserve, about 870,000 acres or 1,350 square miles, is Russia's largest; India's largest tiger park is Kanha, little more than one fourth of that size. Yet Kanha can claim up to 110 resident tigers, as opposed to Sikhote-Alin's twenty to thirty. Tracing old game trails along ridges and in riverbeds, rounding the wooded hills in ceaseless pursuit of elk and boar, male *altaica* are obliged to hunt over a vast territory of 150 square miles (as opposed to the eight square miles estimated for males in Chitwan) to obtain the ten pounds of meat needed each day, and females may cover an area only slightly smaller. Since the female is limited to local hunting when she has cubs hidden nearby, it is not surprising that the reproductive rates of *altaica* in the wild are markedly lower than in *P. t. tigris*, and litter size, too; these northern tigers average 1.7 cubs per litter, compared to 2.8 in both Chitwan and Kanha. Project scientists believe

that such striking discrepancies directly reflect the low prey base of this northern range and the constraints on the tigress's efficient hunting; therefore they believe that a huge area with an undisturbed inner region of at least 400 square miles must be preserved here to support a viable tiger population, since smaller areas tend to have a limited prey base more vulnerable to local hunters.

With a negligible human population and little industry apart from logging and mining, these coastal mountains were by far the largest contiguous region of viable habitat in all of the Asian tiger's range. Using the new GIS maps for its planning, the Siberian Tiger Project was encouraging the acquisition of tracts of this wild land as part of a proposed network of forested areas extending 600 miles, from the northernmost range of the elk and tiger in Khabarovski Krai to the Lazovski Reserve, a small zapovednik on the coast northeast of Vladivostok that I was trying to locate through the plane window. "Lazo" was smaller than the Sikhote-Alin but also better habitat for tigers; with fewer conifers in a more southerly hardwood forest, it supported a denser population of prey animals. Give a tiger good habitat, Howard Quigley says, with something to eat and a way to get there, and it will come.

To avoid the fragmentation and isolation of populations that have taken place in India and elsewhere, the existing reserves would be supplemented by new national parks and also *zakazniks,* or "traditional use" zones, where hunting and gathering are permitted, all of these linked by woodland corridors through the mined and timbered land by which tigers could travel from one habitat area to another. Under the project's proposed plan, the connected habitat, inside the reserves and out, would represent about 27,000 square miles, approximately the size of Florida or Sumatra.

North of "Lazo," off the wingtip, lay the snow peak called Oblachnaya, or Cloud Peak, at 6,083 feet the highest in Sikhote-Alin. On the coast was "Southern Valley," a hunting tract of 640 square miles that is very well situated as a connecting area between protected lands. With help from Save the Tiger Fund, Southern Valley had been leased recently by the project as a quick and innovative means of setting aside critical territory without bureaucratic delays and restoring the elk and wild boar populations for the benefit of hunters as well as tigers.

The mountain valleys opened out at Kavalierova, then the mining settlement at Dalnegorsk—boron and silver, lead and nickel—with its dead piles of mine tailings and settling pools of bad chemical colors. Soon the plane banked east over the sea, dark blue and wind-chopped, with a surf of ice cast up along the shore, then swung back west into the wind for its landing at Plastun, a new port from which truckloads of raw logs of the beautiful Korean pine are shipped out to Japan. This valuable species, which provides cone nuts for the deer and boar, therefore good habitat for tigers, will be the first tree "lumbered out."

From Plastun, the coast road continues north for fifty miles, crossing the southeast part of the reserve before it ends at Terney. North of the reserve there was new logging, and southbound timber trucks stacked high with fir, spruce, and Korean pine were the only vehicles we encountered. The gravel road, paved fitfully here and there according to some scheme that even local people cannot fathom, traverses the mountains in the south part of the reserve, not far inland from the sea, and on the sea side, twenty miles south of Terney, roadside alders climb to a low ridge of oak; west of the road, the woods descend steeply through larch, birch, and poplar to the bottom of the Kunalaika Valley. The valley rises gradually on the far side to long pine ridges, which ascend in turn to the twin snow peaks called the Camel. Here our vehicle stopped on the road shoulder and we got out.

In October 1992, a few months after my first visit, the tigress Lena had grown inactive once again, and it was supposed that she was tending her first litter. In late November, her signal became stationary, and Dale Miquelle, very alarmed, had tracked it to this place across the coast road from the Kunalaika Valley. There he found her collar, slashed from her neck and tossed into the snow by whoever had killed her. Of her young cubs, there was no sign whatever.

As the first "marked" animal to produce a litter, Lena had been critical to many aspects of the tiger study. The heartbroken and enraged Miquelle had rushed back to Terney to report what had happened, and Evgeny Smirnov and Anatoli Astafiev, accompanied by a forest guard and a police officer, returned with him to investigate the poaching site. While they were standing on the road, Smirnov glimpsed a movement in the bushes, and a moment later, four tiger cubs were seen floundering uphill through the snow and alders. Miquelle tore off in pursuit, but was unable to catch them. The unweaned and famished cubs, still waiting for their mother, were keeping faithful vigil at the killing place.

A capture party of nine men was organized at Terney and returned the next morning. As the group moved uphill through the alders, Dale recalled, he struggled to keep the searchers in a line, but the indomitable Russians went haring off as soon as they found a track, and the line disintegrated. Even so, a forest guard soon found two hiding cubs, seizing one up against his chest and shouting for help as he stumbled along in pursuit of the other. By now, Astafiev and his party had come across the third and fourth, backed into a hollow tree. They were duly extricated, with precocious roars and snarling, but not before several of their rescuers had been scratched or bitten. Though only a few weeks old, the cubs were already the size of full-grown bobcats.

Male and female tigers are sexually mature at three to five years, and there are one to four cubs in a litter, though usually only one or two survive to travel with the mother. Two of Lena's cubs would die of genetic abnormalities shortly after capture, but a month later, the two survivors were sent off on a 5,000-mile journey to the United States, accompanied by Drs. Howard and Kathy Quigley. At the Omaha Zoo, they were placed in a captive breeding program for endangered species, and in the spring, the female cub was transferred to Indianapolis, where the zoo staff—to commemorate her mother—named her Lena.

(Among the 1,000-odd tigers that now inhabit the world's zoos, only *altaica* and *tigris* have well-established lineages in captivity; there are far more *altaica* in cages than there are in the Russian Far East. Due to *tigris* charisma and *sapiens* insecurity, thousands of additional tigers of doubtful provenance—zoo culls, circus spitbacks, and the like—dwell in private menageries around the world; an estimated 2,000 of these animals [with about 1,000 lions] reside in Texas, enough for an impressive herd on the King Ranch.)

Maurice Hornocker had made the most of media attention to the orphaned cubs' arrival in the United States to organize financial support for anti-poaching measures in the reserve. At that time, the logging tracks were few, and the projected cost of setting up an effective patrol was about $30,000—$4,000 to $6,000 each for two Russian jeeps plus the very modest salaries of the rangers. The patrols were now in operation, and so far they had been effective, in part because the rangers were accompanied by local policemen with authority to make arrests. No marked tiger had been killed in the reserve since Lena's death in 1992, though others had been shot outside the boundaries.

On our first evening in Terney, a local widow, Emma Alexandrovna, prepared hot borscht and elk dumplings—*pelmeni*—for our supper. The following night I went with Dale to Emma's house to fetch our good dinner of fish soup, elk meatballs, and fiddlehead ferns, gathered last spring and salted and oiled for winter use. Since we dined on elk more evenings than not, I had to wonder how many elk were consumed annually in this community—how many, that is, were being removed from the tiger's prey base all year round.

One evening, on the snowy ridges between Terney and the Kunalaika Valley, we passed three vehicles parked on the shoulder, as pale faces under dark fur hats stared out from the lit cabs. Since night had come, and intense cold, it was not hard to guess why these men seemed to be waiting on the road to no good purpose.

Thanks to the new economic opportunities, Terney had entered a new phase of expansion. Our salmon-fishing friend Volodya Velichko, who had temporarily forsworn vodka, was now the proud capitalist owner of a gas station, and even the beleaguered zapovednik had prospered to a certain extent, with a new building and new computer equipment compatible with the new prestige brought to the reserve by the cooperation and support of the tiger project. The project, in turn, had plainly benefited from the local popularity of Dale Miquelle. As in so many timber towns in America's Pacific Northwest, local hunters and loggers were generally suspicious, even hostile, toward bureaucrats and scientists who might threaten their livelihood, but Dale is good-natured and exuberant and tough in the Russian manner, and Howard Quigley is quiet, humorous, and easygoing, and both men were well liked and trusted. Among the many who greeted them on the street was a young farmer who had lost some stock to depredations of the tigress Olga on a farmstead north of the river but was nonetheless a supporter of the project.

The cottage where we were staying, high on a hill, offered a fine prospect of the frozen Serebryanka, where a tractor was hauling a large cart of cordwood over the ice. Since Arseniev's visit, tides and wind had built up sand, turning the bay into a lagoon. High dunes had formed on the north side, but the sea was visible between dune and headland at the river mouth.

Howard Quigley pointed out the low place between dunes within sight of the village, where Olga—Tiger #1—had been captured at the outset of the project. The year before, when her radio batteries wore out, she had to be recaptured in a helicopter foray, a process that so enraged her that she climbed into a tree and clawed the air to fight off the machine and its fearful racket. (In these recaptures, the ma-

chine must hover while the dart is placed and the drugged tiger reels and sags onto the ground, after which the biologists are lowered by light cable, hoping the patient remains comatose long enough to get the job done. As Quigley says, "That is not an adventure for the faint-hearted," a phrase which might describe the entire project.)

In his office at reserve headquarters, I renewed acquaintance with Evgeny Smirnov, who showed me a tiger skull with a smashed jaw. Apparently this animal, stalking a horse in its corral at the edge of the village, had had a canine, an incisor, and a small bone broken by a flying hoof. Even so, it persisted in its horse hunting, and in mid-April 1985, Evgeny said, it had attacked a ranger's horse within the village. Chased off by gunfire, it attempted to flee across the Sere-bryanka and fell through the spring ice. Its carcass was recovered when the ice went out about two weeks later.

Dr. Smirnov was drinking tea that afternoon in November 1992 when Miquelle rushed in with the bad news that he'd found Lena's slashed collar in the snow near the coast road. "If I had a license to kill Lena's poacher, I would do it," Smirnov said grimly, more than three years after the event. "I would enjoy fulfilling such a duty."

In July 1993, a local wildlife official named Victor Naumenko had been caught with a tiger skin and convicted of poaching, yet was promptly let off with a suspended sentence and rehired by the Hunting Department as a conservation officer responsible for the control of poaching. Smirnov believes that over 95 percent of the tiger poaching was perpetrated from the roads, usually by part-time hunters and logging truck drivers on the lookout for elk and other game. A small man with a dour face and sudden smile, he added thoughtfully, "I'd shoot that kind, too. Better a true poacher than a person with responsibility for conservation." Because villagers had told them that Naumenko had boasted of the deed, Smirnov and Miquelle were persuaded that this man was Lena's killer, but they also realized that in this hard economy, neither the police nor the judiciary was very interested.

Having heard that a new Russian group called Phoenix was being set up to take over environmental duties, I asked if the Russians would continue the tiger project after the Americans went home. Smirnov shrugged. "We would like to continue but first we must change the way things are. There are no drugs now for the hospitals, let alone for immobilizing tigers," he said wryly. And after all, these magnificent creatures had become the responsibility of the whole world, like the Sikhote-Alin and Lake Baikal, which had been recognized as "international biosphere reserves." If it was to succeed, he said, the project would require ongoing support from America and other enlightened nations.

A cold clear daybreak, −4°F. Frozen smoke from a few village chimneys rose against the dark headland of the cliffs as I fetched split logs for our stove and a bucket of water from the pump. The outhouse, despite its stirring view downriver to the sea, was no place for dawdlers in the Siberian winter. But the little house was warm enough, and soon a cold sun rose from Japan, casting a pewter glaze on the rigid river.

At the airstrip, I recognized the crude old AN-2 biplane, faded gray and orange—the sort of crate one might expect to see belly-deep in scrub and weeds off the far end of the farthest Third World airstrip. After strenuous heating by a hot-air blower on the ground, the frozen engine kicked sluggishly and turned over, and the wind and cold accompanied us into its bare metal cabin as, with a great roar, it zigzagged down the airstrip. Inside, the shuddering machine seemed even slower and more noisy than in 1992, and very much colder, too, but it was airborne, more or less—we were aloft. Valeri, the pilot, climbed to a few thousand feet, to make sure none of the tiger signals would be cut off by the mountains, then turned south down the coast toward Blogovatna, a lovely lake behind the dunes where in those cool early-summer days of 1992 I had walked the woods and beach and sea cliffs, looking for birds.

The nine "marked" tigers were monitored biweekly from the air, to make sure they were still alive and still transmitting. All but two were female, which was to be expected. Cubs are divided more or less equally between the sexes, but by adulthood, there are apt to be two to four females for each male. This is because the females remain longer with their mothers, then establish themselves not far away in familiar territory, whereas a young male, striking out into unknown, hostile country toward the end of his second year, encounters considerably more risk from hunters and poachers in addition to accidents or injury due to inexperience in making a kill; in attempting to take over a territory and acquire the females whose home ranges that territory overlaps, he must often fight an older, larger male, sustaining injuries that may be fatal.

Tiger #5—the tigress Katia—which had taken over Lena's range two years after her death, had recently been frequenting Blogovatna.

So had Tiger #9, a male named Geny, who had been spending too much time in the environs of Terney, making no one happy. It appeared that Katia had been bred by Geny, who had been with her over a three-day period in early December, a liaison discovered because the pair remained close to the road and were exceptionally noisy—not uncommon among tigers in the throes of mating. To protect them against poachers, the project's new researchers, a young couple named John Goodrich and Linda Kerley, had monitored their caterwauling. Later they were threatened by Katia, when they inadvertently approached her den site in the Kumami drainage; she backed off only when met with a cloud of pepper spray of the sort used in North America to discourage bears. Apparently Katia had lost a first litter to disease or weakness, or to wolves, lynx, bears, or other predators that discovered the den, or to another tiger.

Because his large territory is hard to defend, a male may be driven off by a stronger male after only two or three years; females persist on their territories longer. In a good prey area, under normal conditions, a tigress may produce a litter every two or three years, but when a new male takes over in her home territory, he may kill his predecessor's young in order to bring the tigress into estrus eight months faster; in this way, most male carnivores—and primates, too—clear the way for their own genes as soon as possible, before they are killed or driven off by new contenders. (In monogamous species, which mostly bond for life, the male may devote his energies to helping protect and rear the young instead of eating them.)

Katia's signals were coming from farther west in the Kunalaika Valley, just below the place on the coast road where Lena had been killed. The plane descended into the river bottoms, which were mostly open, scattered with large cottonwoods and birch and poplar, a few spruce, yet scanning from a slow airplane, often no more than 300 feet above the ground, we were unable to find her. With Dale at his elbow, our dauntless pilot made eight or ten close passes, throttling the clanking engine down to a near-stall, so that the vibrating hulk seemed to shudder to a dead halt in midair; he abandoned this folly only when the ancient machine, carving the valley side too close, collided with its own prop wash and was jarred heavily toward the wooded slope. At last the good Valeri had had enough, for the plane roared up and out of the Kunalaika.

Having apparently bred Katia, Geny had left the Terney region and moved far south across the snowbound ridges. The close proximity of their signals told us that he was presently attending Tiger #3 (Natasha) and her two grown cubs, who would probably disperse on their own later this spring. The four tigers were hidden in a grove of spruce in a snowy hollow, and despite all of Valeri's inspired maneuvers, we did not see them. I began to fear that luck was not with us and we would see no tigers.

The plane banked south and west, leaving the reserve as it crossed the Djigit River, then circled back over a tributary stream where Dale picked up a signal. Crisscrossing the valley, it made a wide turn over a logging track, and there I saw the first wild tiger of my life, bounding across the white expanse in bursts of powder. With the low winter sun glancing off the snow, all I could see was that black, bounding silhouette. The image evoked a Tungus belief that stalking tigers use the sun to blind their prey, leaping out of that wild fireball at dawn or sunset like a tongue of flame.

Crossing the track, the tiger plunged toward a big solitary spruce. Yelling at Howard, who turned in time to see it, I jumped up to the cockpit to point out its location to Dale and Valeri. Our intrepid aviator hurled the last scrap of his prudence to the skies, circling the spruce tighter and tighter, as if intent on vanishing in a tight columnar blur of motor oil, much as those circling tigers in *Little Black Sambo* had dissolved in a golden ring of fine ghee butter. But Tiger #21, the tigress Nadia, had abandoned that lone tree and was making a run for a nearby grove of conifers, for on a turn, as the plane banked across the treetops, I saw the warm burnt-orange creature moving toward me among the sunlit evergreens on the white snow. Feeling herself hidden, or at least safe, she did not bother to look up or turn aside, but moved ahead, intent on her own path, on the sparkling white corridor between the pines. Then the plane was past and she was gone and I sat back sighing, with a vast grin of well-being.

Tiger #12, a 400-pound male (called Dale after Dr. Miquelle),

was located in a birch copse on a high rock pinnacle. Having no place to run, he must have been lying motionless on the sunny snow, gazing with hauteur at the old airplane that lumbered past at eye level, spoiling his lordly view. Once again, despite Valeri's crazed efforts, we did not spot him in the sparse cover of small trees, and so we turned back toward the north part of the reserve, where Tiger #4 (Maria Ivanovna, also referred to as Marijuana, or Nirvana) was usually found just outside the boundary. Where ravens scattered she appeared to have a kill, but Marijuana was not seen, and neither was Olga, who was accompanied these days by a female cub. The old biplane returned south, passing offshore of the rock coast where, in 1992, Maurice Hornocker and I, fishing for pink salmon with Volodya, had seen two goral on the sea cliffs. (Since then, at the Lazovski Reserve, a pair of goral had been blasted off the cliffs by seagoing poachers using automatic weapons.)

At seven next morning, when we left Terney with Anatoli Astafiev, the coast range was still locked in bitter darkness, and an hour later, though the sun had tipped the treetops on the cliff with ragged fire, the air remained transfixed by Arctic cold.

For the past three years, Astafiev had sought to add to the reserve a 130,000-acre tract in the mountains to the west. Because the Siberian Tiger Project had assisted in this effort by helping to organize its financing abroad, Anatoli had arranged a visit to the new extension, which would give us an opportunity to talk with concerned foresters and local people of the high-country logging village of Melnichnoye, where the local economy might be affected, and try to combat a prevailing misconception that the tigers were in fatal competition with the local hunters.

At the Djigit River, a road that leads west over the mountains toward the Ussuri Valley follows the southwestern boundary of the reserve in a gradual ascent into higher, colder country. According to a demographic map on the wall of our cottage, this region of Ussuri Land, like most of Siberia, had a population density of 0 to 1 human being per square mile. On the four-hour journey from Terney to Melnichnoye, not a single sign of human habitation broke the great expanse of forest. Drab winter finches flitted across white road and river like blown chips of bark, and a squirrel with exquisite ear tassels sprang up onto a snowbank and whisked down again.

Turning off on a woodland trail into the reserve, Astafiev told us that this side canyon shelters giant rhododendron as big as trees—the only range of this archaic plant besides a few small pockets in North Korea and Japan. In the canyon, three rangers of the anti-poaching patrol were bivouacked in a log cabin set in a grove of fir and spruce. Twisting the bright orange cones among white snowcaps on the fir tops was a flock of crossbills, the males a burning-ember red and black, their mates flame yellow.

The previous night the rangers had chased a poacher until after 1 a.m. Though they gave the driver a citation and confiscated a jack light, they had failed to catch the rifleman, who had run away into the woods. Periodically he would reappear along the wood edge, then dart back among the trees when they came after him. The rangers had the satisfaction of knowing how cold their quarry must have been, but they had to admit that he was a tough customer, for when they first saw him, he was riding on top of the car, clutching his rifle in the night wind of subzero weather.

We breakfasted heavily on bread and potatoes, with fine cold crabmeat and half-raw salmon *gorbusha* and the delicious herring-like *korbushka* fished up through the ice of the Serebryanka, and also yellow cheese and tea and the gaudily wrapped plastic-colored candies that are as ubiquitous as metal teeth here in Siberia. One of the forest guards was Rudolf Judt. Asked where he got his German name, he smiled and said, "That's a long story. We'd have to go all the way back to Catherine the Great." I apologized for my nosy questions, assuring them I was not from the KGB. The guards laughed, and one cried out, "We are not afraid, not anymore!"

Then we were off again, crossing the coast range's low divide, 2,400 feet above the sea. As usual, the only vehicles we spotted on the

road were the great logging trucks bound for the timber export depot at Plastun. One truck was stalled on an uphill grade, and another had overturned, dumping its cargo. No doubt the trucks would remain right there until winter eased its iron grip and their rock-hard engines could be started.

By midmorning, still headed west, we were crossing the high central plateaus, where the mountain air bit at the face like an ice tiger. Game tracks wandered everywhere among the snowy firs and bone-white birches, and we chased from the roadside a young elk, woolly-brown in its thick winter coat. It struggled away over a rocky knoll, up to its brisket in the snow. The ungulates, and the tigers, too, have difficulty in deep snow—one reason why the tiger favors forest avenues made by the wild boar and why it makes use of man-made tracks like the coast road where it is most in danger.

Anatoli pointed out with pride the mountain landmarks of the new reserve addition, which includes the headwaters of the Kolumbey River. The critical protection of the upper Kolumbey within the reserve boundaries was part of Anatoli's vision, Howard Quigley says. Soon the road crossed the river, which traverses a high plain. Near Melnichnoye, the river joins the Bolshaya Ussurka (Big Small Ussuri), which descends westward to the Ussuri and the Amur, arriving eventually at the Sea of Okhotsk, a thousand miles off to the north.

The Kolumbey is broader and slower than the steeper torrents of the eastern slope, which plunge directly to the Japan Sea, but in the spring it may overflow that part of the village that lies below the higher ground of the old settlement. When Arseniev rode through here almost a century ago, this village was called Tsidatun—Chinese for "windy valley." In those days it was a settlement of native Udege and also some Manchurian Chinese, and even today a few mixed-blood aboriginals may still be found here. Ever since the days of the Chinese, there has been a gold mine up the river, and it still employed about fifty local people.

The community's head forester, Nikolai Andreev Kosichko, welcomed us into his small house at the west end. An iron-haired man with melancholy eyes, he remarked upon this balmy winter weather, noting that the other day the temperature had fallen to −36°F. Kosichko observed that until 1971, the scattering of peasant cottages and sheds on this flat river plain between low ridges had remained "a pure forest village, and everybody was a hunter and trapper, with scarcely 150 people altogether." ("Yes, they were all hunters out in the taiga," Anatoli agreed, "and you rarely saw one.") Then logging arrived, first a state-run enterprise and now a private timber company. By 1985, the village population had grown to five times its former size, and today there were approximately 1,000 souls.

Forestry at Melnichnoye was based on selective cutting (the community rejected clear-cuts after just one try). "Our logging laws—how to cut trees and manage the forests—would be fine if they could be enforced, but they are not. No money. The Korean pine is mostly gone, and now the company is taking spruce high on the slopes, causing erosion. And since we have no agricultural prospects, we do not know what will become of us." The forester looked bleakly from one face to another. There had been talk of a "half-factory" to do the first rough stages of wood processing, but nothing had come of it, as usual.

Outside his house was a stack of lumber from trees trucked down the mountains to Plastun for some rough cutting, then shipped back here for local use, a 170-mile round trip. "But most of our timber is shipped out through Plastun, and almost no benefit comes back to our community," Kosichko said. "We are supposed to receive 30 percent of any profit, but the federal government takes 80 percent and local officials take the other 20. We can't expect help from those officials, who have plenty of problems of their own—which is to say, no money."

As we talked, men and women came in to hear the conversation. Forest guard Vladimir Sharov, a handsome man in green camouflage uniform whose bushy eyebrows, sideburns, and black beard gave him a passing resemblance to Fidel Castro, said that local sentiment ran strongly against the reserve and its new extension, and against the village forest guard in consequence. He offered a fine metallic smile. "Life is very different now. It's not just the economy. Everyone is living for the moment and looking out only for themselves. Our life is out of control—it's chaos." I heard this refrain repeatedly in the new Russia. Before their world changed in 1989, there was an

environmental-education program in the village, and tree planting, too. "That's all gone now. Before, the people volunteered to help, out of enthusiasm. Today, nobody will lift a finger unless they are given money."

"Well, at least children don't think that way. They think from the heart!" a woman cried, as if trying to persuade herself that this was so.

"Why do those Japanese demand our Korean pine when they know that cutting that kind of pine is now illegal?" Maria Kosichko complained rhetorically, only to be teased by her husband's assistant,

Sergei Zinoviev, a balding man with a beard and a sly humor. "If the Japanese ask for our Korean pine, we cut our pine, and if the Chinese need our tiger bones, we shoot our tigers! It's not *our* fault!" And Katia Sharov, in a red sweater, laughed, crying out ruefully, "We have a democracy in Russia now! No rules at all!"

If the villagers had mixed feelings about the reserve, they also had ambivalence about the tiger. The previous winter, a Melnichnoye trapper named Sergei Denisov, aged thirty-seven, had been killed and eaten by a tiger, leaving a widow and two children. No, Sergei had not made some blunder. "There is a critical distance with a tiger. He walked within it—that was that," said Vladimir Sharov, who had been the dead man's friend. "Sergei did not intend to harm the tiger, therefore he made no mistake." Anyway, Sergei Denisov had not been the first tiger victim in Melnichnoye. In 1958—the villagers consulted on this date—the head of the local weather station had been taken.

In Dersu's time, Amba had been revered as "the True Spirit of the Mountains," a wilderness deity and fearsome guardian of the precious ginseng root; these days, the True Spirit of the Mountains was spoken of offhandedly as Koschka, the Cat. The word *Amba* is no longer used, nor have the villagers retained any Udege myths about the forest. "We have the Russian outlook now," Nikolai Andreevich said.

Asked if the community would be better off if the last tigers were exterminated, the villagers gave a heartfelt groan of assent. But almost immediately Sharov protested that the taiga would be "boring" without tigers, and Sergei Zinoviev agreed. He granted that fewer tigers might be better, since the game animals that tigers killed were badly needed by the community. "But for me," he said, "life is more interesting with tigers around, although most people here would never miss them." Even the women spoke up to discount any threat to people in the village, although ten years earlier—the same hard winter when four separate tigers had prowled Vladivostok—one had entered the dirt lanes between these cottages, devoured a dog, and mauled a colt.

Anyway, Zinoviev said, a man should not go into the taiga if he is afraid. All summer, he and other local gatherers of ginseng and wild foods walked the forest without guns, which were carried only in the hunting season. Zinoviev was the head of the local hunting club, which leased the flora and fauna—in effect, the right to hunt and gather—on 700 square miles of land that adjoined the reserve addition. Unlike most such hunting groups, his club favored the proposed land acquisition, confident that the protected animals would overflow into its leased land. Zinoviev hoped that the wild harvest on this land—Siberian ginseng, mushrooms and berries, wild honey, ferns, and medicinal plants—would pay the lease fees, but he wondered where what was gathered could be sold. There was no Chinese market for Siberian ginseng or for ginseng grown domestically; all the Chinese would accept was the wild plant, a red-berried aralia whose man-shaped root descends a foot or more into the earth and is sometimes worth more than a thousand dollars. Unfortunately, wild ginseng was now so scarce that the annual harvest in Primorski Krai had a legal limit of sixty-six pounds. The previous year, only seventeen pounds was sold—legally, that is. Now that the borders had been opened, there was no telling how much wild ginseng would be dug and smuggled out for private sale.

These days, the fine for shooting tigers was a million rubles, or two hundred times the state minimum salary, and half of that again for selling tiger parts. Not that a man would be sent to prison for failure to pay the fine, he would only have most of his belongings confiscated. "If you're going to save tigers," Zinoviev said, "you have to have stiffer penalties or provide a better life. If people could make a decent living, they would not shoot tigers."

Anyway, the tiger was no longer poached much for its hide and bones because the trade was being closed down by the antipoaching patrol along the Plastun road, formerly a favorite haunt of gun traders and hunters, and by the replacement of corrupt customs officials on the borders. Zinoviev astonished us by adding that tigers these days were mostly killed for food. "A third of the people in this room have eaten tiger, though they might not admit it," Zinoviev said. He pointed at a ridge north of the village. "A tiger used to travel along that hillside. Somebody saw him every year. But we don't see him anymore, because we ate him." Tiger meat was like pork, he added, but leaner, lighter. "Want to try some?" Everybody laughed. The humor seemed less ironic than profoundly rueful, fatalistic. Later I asked Anatoli if this sly fellow had been fooling us. Astafiev shook his head. Maybe Zinoviev had exaggerated—tiger meat was not to every taste—but yes, some people ate tiger, that was true.

For all their gloomy predictions about the future, most Russians, in the back country at least, remain eager and hospitable. Sure enough, they had prepared a fine elk feast in honor of the visitors. "Russians have to grow and hunt all their own food," Zinoviev said. "Almost everything on this table was provided by ourselves except for the *kohlbasa*, and nobody is eating that stuff, have you noticed? In the old days, we had to be self-sufficient, too, but at least we were able to put something aside in case we had to travel, to pay our respects at our grandmother's funeral or something. Today such a journey is no longer possible."

In Vladimir Sharov's opinion, most of the resistance to the zapovednik and its new extension comes from the tree-cutters, some of whom Zinoviev dismissed as "bums out for a free ride"—the same element, someone called out during our banquet, who voted for "that clown Zhirinovsky" in the last election. As tall black Americans ranged back and forth across the small TV screen, shooting astonishing flying baskets, we drank schnapps toasts and consumed a variety of fish and crab, Siberian dumplings and pickled tomatoes, chicken salad, a fine elk plate with carrots and potatoes, and also something very good called "overcoat," which turned out to be a fine hot fish suited up in beets and mashed potatoes. For dessert, there were dishes of superb wildflower honey for which the villagers could no longer find a market.

The Melnichnoyans spoke with tolerance of Mikhail Gorbachev, in a country in which *perestroika* is a dirty word: "He meant well, but he had no means to implement his reforms, so he just brought trouble." As for Yeltsin, "He started well, but already he is finished." As for Chechnya, "That mess could not have happened in the Soviet days, we can tell you that much!" But Nikolai Andreevich cut all this off, out of courtesy to his guests. "Let's not talk about it," he said gloomily. "Let's stick to our own problems. The state has problems and we have problems. We lived poorly in the past and we will have to live poorly in the future. That is Russia."

Vladimir Sharov led us to the house of the late Sergei Denisov's hunting partner, a woolly-headed young man with a muffled voice whose stunned demeanor could not be entirely attributed to his shocking experience of the year before. "Sasha" described how he and Denisov and Denisov's brother-in-law Sergei Polishuk had been hunting and trapping on a tributary stream of the Kolumbey. On February 14, 1995, Denisov, who had gone upstream to check his sable traps, failed to return. On the sixteenth, Polishuk went out to look for him, and that same day, Sharov had come through on his patrol, staying overnight in the trappers' cabin. Returning on the seventeenth, Polishuk told them that all he'd found was a pair of legs and a few red traces in the snow, surrounded by the pugmarks of a tigress.

Knowing the tigress would not have strayed far from those legs, Polishuk fired a shot to keep her at a distance, then fled back to the cabin, where he told Sasha and the forest guard what had happened.

The three came back to Melnichnoye to notify the police, then accompanied the officials to the death scene, some thirty miles northeast of the village. By that time, the legs had disappeared, but they found the larger pugmarks of a male tiger that had come along later and sniffed out the scene.

On the twenty-first, project researcher Igor Nikolaev came to investigate, accompanied by Dale Miquelle. (Because Igor is widely respected in Primorski Krai, his conclusions would be acceptable as the official report.) Though the original tracks were now quite old, and had been obscured by light fresh snow as well as by the tracks of the male tiger, this quiet man as brown as a woodland leaf went to work with a pine whisk, uncovering sign. The man-eater, he said, had been half-starved, not simply because she had attacked a man but because the whitish color of her scat identified an animal that had eaten insufficiently for a long time.

The tigress had lain in a sheltered bed under the base of a fallen tree, and had gathered herself for an attack when she heard something approaching. The point where the trapper had turned his back on her to leave his path and make his way around the tip of the fallen tree was perhaps eight yards from her place of shelter, and he was just twelve yards away, Nikolaev determined, when she leapt and struck him.

Denisov's mittens lay five steps from the blood traces on the snow, and the upper barrel of his fallen rifle, an over-and-under single shot used for squirrels or birds or rabbits, was still loaded and the hammer cocked. It appeared he had removed his gloves to fire at small game, and that in bending over to lay them down, momentarily resembling a prey animal, he might well have triggered her attack. (A Ranthambhore tigress that lay peacefully for hours while being filmed by Belinda Wright had stalked her scarily as soon as Belinda stepped aside to crouch down in the bushes.) Had the trapper seen the tigress, he probably would have stood his ground and shouted, perhaps fired off his gun, and in all likelihood that would have spared his life. But to the end he remained unaware of her, to judge from the absence of any sign of flight or struggle. Except for one shocked instant of wild pain and terror, he probably never quite realized his life was ending.

Sergei Denisov had been killed in the new reserve extension about four miles north of the Kolumbey. Furthermore, it was possible although unlikely that the male that happened on the scene was a project tiger; the local people could not have known that a radio-collared tiger—the big male, #4, nicknamed Kolya—might have wandered west to the Kolumbey headwaters. In any case, it seemed important to stifle local rumors about marked tigers before people concluded that, maddened by their collars, they became prone to man-eating behavior. Igor Nikolaev was glad he could establish that the man-eater in this case had been an unknown female. Unfortunately, she was never caught.

Denisov's hunting partner felt no resentment of the reserve and its new addition—"Let it stay." Nor did he express fear or bitterness about the tigers. He shrugged, fatalistic. "Let them be," he said. As far as he knew, Denisov's brother-in-law Sergei Polishuk felt the same way. On this frozen day in January, in fact, Polishuk was "out there in the forest" where he belonged.

On the four-hour return to Terney on the mysterious white road through the mountain darkness, I kept an eye out for the night hunters, but the only creature abroad in such great cold was a gray dark-eyed Ural owl, crouched by a snowbank with its rodent prey. The owl did not fly, only turned its head when the small auto rushed past. On frozen nights, the predators are bold and do not readily give up their kill.

The following day, in the afternoon, we stopped again on the icebound empty road where Lena's collar had been found. Here the tigress Katia had adopted Lena's habit of hiding her litter in a den east of the road and crossing it to hunt in the Kunalaika. Not fifty yards from where Lena had been killed—and this seemed eerie in these miles of empty road—we found Katia's tracks in the deep snow where she had come down from the ridge and

crossed the road to descend to the elk bottoms. Her radio signal—a
pulsing beat like the hard chipping of a bird, or like the rubbing of
two stones together—was loud and fast, though this might have been
caused by the chafing of her collar on a frozen kill.

A tigress with cubs has an easier time in winter when the bears
are hibernating; brown bears and black are plentiful in these forests,
and twelve browns and nine blacks have been caught in the snares
since the project started in 1992. While it is thought that an adult
tiger will drive off all but a large male brown, a female with cubs is at
great disadvantage. Bears emerging from their dens after hibernation
will track tigers in order to steal their kills, and the project has many
records of large bears usurping kills before and after the tiger makes
its meal. That tigers usually guard their kills until the meat is gone

frustrates the bears, to judge from the fact that kills are sometimes splattered with bear feces. (The large project tiger nicknamed Dale dined regularly on bears, which constituted the bulk of his peculiar diet.) Since tigers require a medium-sized prey animal each week, and a tigress with cubs even more, bear competition is especially unwelcome, since appropriation of her hard-earned kill will oblige her to keep hunting all the harder, perhaps at a dangerous distance from the den.

To verify the existence of Katia's litter, we wanted to check the tiger tracks around the kill. While she was present, we could not go down there, not wishing to disturb the tigress and her cubs (nor take that risk). People investigating kills to scavenge meat or even venturing too close cause the tigress to abandon the kill about 60 percent of the time; this, too, forces her to hunt more often. Even hikers and fishermen, passing by, disturb her. And so we went south to the Djigit River and followed the trans-montane road to the Sheptoon Valley, where I had seen the tigress Nadia from the airplane two days before.

Along the logging road into that valley were myriad fresh tracks—elk and a much smaller deer, a roe or sika, and squirrel and hare and mink, and perhaps sable, together with fresh tracks of a male tiger. (The sex can be determined by the larger size of the pad width of the forepaw, which in this case was four inches across; a younger male with a print of female size—three and a half inches or smaller—would still be accompanied by the mother.) The pugmarks left the logging road at a point where this unknown male had inspected a leaning tree for another's scent marks. Farther on, either this animal or Nadia had left a urine trace out on the logging track. At the recommendation of my companions, I knelt and gave this mark a sniff. In the frozen air, its strong acids were bracing.

Because the snow was too deep for the vehicle, we trekked the last half mile to the place where Nadia had gone bounding across the track toward the shelter of a grove of spruce and pine. In the deep snow, her tracks continued eastward, pausing between two close-set spruce trunks (as if she had sought cover when the plane roared low), then continuing onward toward the steep wall of the valley. In one place the tigress had stretched out, melting the snow; a red spot in the glaze of ice was sign of a cut paw. (The pads of tigers are so sensitive that the thin skin is often lacerated by broken ice.)

Though Nadia, five to six years old, was fully mature, she was not known to have had a litter and might not have mated. For the first time, said reserve assistant Alyosha Kostnya, a skilled tracker who had helped with Nadia's capture in this drainage in December, her radio signal could not be picked up from the ground. She had departed her home valley, and possibly that unknown male was with her.

That evening toward dusk, Katia recrossed the road and climbed the eastern ridge, apparently on her way back to her litter (as it turned out, there was just one cub, which she would bring across the road a few days later). The next morning her signal, coming from the ridge east of the road, indicated she was resting, and so we descended through the hillside woods to find her kill. In the deep frost, a pea-green moth cocoon, suspended from a twig, was the solitary note of green in the rigid forest.

The snow in the woods was two feet deep and fluffy with dry

cold, but in the bottoms, we could walk the smooth white surface of the Kunalaika, which in this place was forty feet across. On the river ice, most of the snow had been taken by the wind, and the pugmarks were crisp, as if incised in steel. In one place the tigress had lain down and stretched, leaving behind a ghostly outline of the True Spirit of the Mountains, even to the big head and long tail, the leg crook, the big floppy paws. All that was missing was the stripes.

Her ambush place was on a river island of small bent saplings, black against the snow—uncanny camouflage for the white accents of her mask as well as her vertical black streakings. Not far away, the heart-shaped prints of a young elk broke the ice glaze on an oxbow off the river, and from snow evidence, we were able to reconstruct just what had happened. The foreprints came together where the elk stopped short in a place of elm and cottonwood, some seventy yards from the crouched tiger. (The great cats have never adapted to their own strong smell by learning to hunt upwind when stalking—one reason they miss at least nine kills out of ten. Lions have never evolved this instinct either, but at least they have the advantage of group effort.)

Perhaps the elk twitched pink-lined ears and listened, perhaps it sniffed and trembled for a moment, big dark eyes round. From this taut point it suddenly sprang sideways, attaining the far bank in one scared bound as the tigress launched herself from hiding and cut across her quarry's route in ten-foot leaps, leaving silent round explosions in the snow. Shooting through the dark riverine trees like a tongue of fire, she overtook the big deer and hauled it down in a wood of birch and poplar about thirty-seven yards—Dale walked it off—from where she'd started. The tiger, striking from behind, may bite through the vertebrae at the nape or (as in this case) grasp the throat to suffocate its prey. There was little blood, only the arc where

a bony deer leg had swept a weak half circle in the white dust of the snow, and a last sad spasm of pale yellow urine.

With logging trucks howling down the coast road no more than sixty yards away up the steep slope, the woodland stream was much too close to man, and so the tigress with uncanny strength had picked up the elk behind the head and lugged it some ninety yards farther to the west, across the oxbow and over the swamp island where she had lain in hiding. Seeing the smooth drag mark with its spots of blood, I imagined unwillingly the similar track left by the body of poor Sergei Denisov, the lolling head brushing the snow and the final astonishment in the wide eyes.

The elk's carcass had been dropped beneath a thick-trunked alder with dry catkins. Here the cat had fed before moving it farther to a wiry thicket at the edge of swampy meadow scattered with birch and hawthorn and a woody rose, the better to protect it from such scavengers as the raven and raccoon dog and the sea eagles—the white-tailed eagle and the Steller's, with its brutal yellow beak. Almost certainly she had been hidden in this cover when our old biplane had come roaring over a few days before. And having seen this place of crystalline silence in the winter forest, I understood much better how the Russian researchers, before radio telemetry came to Primorski Krai, had learned so much about *P. t. altaica* by reading signs of life and death in the winter taiga.

Not far away, along the dragging track, were the tigress's redoubtable defecations. Delighted by what he called the clearest and most classic kill among the hundred-odd he had inspected, Dale pointed out that she had hardly left her lair except to go relieve herself, which was why no detail of this ambush, kill, and feeding had been obscured. "Can you imagine," he exclaimed, "what this place would look like if a human hunter had lived here for four days?" Of the young elk, all that remained were the legs and head and stiff coarse hide, which are usually abandoned by the tiger. There was no meat left on the twisted carcass. Even the eyes were frozen to blue ice, too hard for ravens.

Down the road on foot came Victor Voronin, a forest guard who is posted at the cabin near the sea at Blogovatna. Voronin claims more close encounters with the tiger than anybody in the Terney region, and he has spoken publicly against the Siberian Tiger Project, objecting to the stress inflicted by the snaring and the indignity of a radio collar on a wild animal. He says correctly but naïvely that intrusive methods would be quite unnecessary if people would only deal with tigers as respectfully as he does. But of course few share his reverence for tigers, far less his sangfroid, and anyway, it seems idle to fuss at careful research methods that might help spare a beautiful animal extinction in the wild.

Voronin greeted the researchers warmly, as if chagrined that his carping statements have distanced him from project people and even fellow staff members on the reserve. Like all forest guards, he carried a rifle—for defense against poachers, Victor claimed, although most guards readily acknowledge that the rifle was a precaution against bears and tigers. He had walked the forest all day long, seeing very few *ezuber* (elk), he informed Dale. His unshaved face was red with cold, and he grinned a cheerful, gat-toothed grin, saying his mouth was so stiff-frozen that he could not talk.

Over the night, the temperature had fallen to −17°F and the next morning the north wind was blowing frozen air at twenty miles an hour. Plastun reported that the airplane for Vladivostok would depart at 11:45 a.m., but at 11:25, from the coast road, we saw that it was already on the airstrip. By the time we got there a few minutes later, the pilot had decided to depart early and was already moving down the runway. Bounding from the car, Dale rushed inside, where the airport manager cried, "Too late!" Undaunted, he ran upstairs to the control room and commanded the radio operator to notify the pilot that the missing passengers had arrived on time. "Send 'em out, then!" yelled the pilot, and a moment later our van hurtled down the runway as if seeking to obliterate the silver jet that churned up clouds of frozen snow as it gunned its motors down at the far end. We jumped aboard and were suddenly aloft, and nobody bothered to check our seat belts or inspect our tickets.

In the terminal at Vladivostok, two dwarf women were squalling at each other in deep hideous voices. Heavily bundled and dead drunk, they grappled and fell to the floor as soft as powder puffs, and one poured her open beer bottle over the other, who sat up weeping. Outside, our driver had a copy of *Peter the Great* in the front seat. The devil-may-care airline pilot, the drunken dwarfs, the student of Czar Peter—such people offered fine instruction about Russia, a country of resolute folly like our own.

In Vladivostok, I spoke with Victor Korkishko, director of the small reserve called Kedrovya Pad, in that region of the East Manchurian Mountains which borders China's Jilin Province. Only twelve miles west of Vladivostok across the frozen bay, Kedrovya Pad (which has since become a research station of the tiger project) had occasional tigers and at least a few Amur or Far Eastern leopards, which formerly ranged from the southern valleys of Primorski Krai south and east into Manchuria and the Koreas. The Far Eastern leopard is now all but extinct in China, but Korkishko thinks there might be ten to fifteen in Ussuria and thirty to forty more in North Korea; the creature is even closer to extinction than the Amur tiger.

The previous summer, with tiger researchers Igor Nikolaev and

Dimitri Pikunov, Korkishko had searched for evidence of tigers across the Chinese border in Heilongjiang. Dr. Pikunov was convinced that no tiger could survive in that battered landscape; any tigers that might occur there were border wanderers "on their way back to Russia." The soft-spoken Korkishko, less adamant than Pikunov, had noted the good condition of the forests, where the main timber tree is the Korean pine. The logging there was partially restricted, with encouraging reforestation, and no sign of fires. However, the Russian team could find just one set of pugmarks, a male tiger, and was disturbed by the low density of the prey species.

While in Heilongjiang, the Russians met a wildlife official from Jilin Province who claimed that Jilin had "about thirty leopards and some tigers." They did not believe him, and I understood why. Traveling by air from Harbin to Beijing on my way to Mongolia in 1992, I had studied many square miles of Jilin landscape on a clear bright morning and saw nothing but an unbroken tapestry of red brick towns and pale green agriculture, all but treeless. Nevertheless, a UN-sponsored survey co-led by Dale Miquelle in 1997 would discover evidence of four to six tigers in a forested region of Jilin near the Russian border, despite that same low density of prey. The project has encouraged the Jilin officials to protect and monitor the prey species and to support what might conceivably develop into a small breeding population of *altaica.*

In March 1998, on a second Jilin survey undertaken with WCS, Miquelle and his party covered 155 miles of pre-selected survey routes in bottomlands, creeks, and frozen rivers, old logging roads, ridges, and divides, all of which serve as pathways for wild animals. Signs of four to six tigers and four to seven leopards were recorded, but no cub prints were found, nor any other evidence of reproduction.

More than fifty wire snares were found along the routes, five with dead deer in them; though some of these seemed long abandoned, they were still catching deer. The team calculated that these rusting snares might be killing about 2,000 ungulates each year in this one county.

While project researchers still believe in those four to six tigers that left tracks in Heilongjiang, a survey in the winter of 1999 in the Wandushan Mountains, which Dale calls "the stronghold of tigers in northeastern China," was unable to locate a single tiger track, despite excellent tracking conditions; one recalls with misgivings those twelve tigers in western Java that died out within a single decade, unassisted on their way by human beings. The local Chinese still report that tigers (including what they think might be a breeding female) continue to occur in Heilongjiang but "noting this one exception," says Miquelle, "the Amur tiger is 'technically' extinct in China, since there is no reproduction, and all evidence suggests that the animals counted earlier dispersed from Russia. Northeast China has great potential habitat but it is filled with snares, eliminating prey and making forests uninhabitable for tigers. If they can protect the forests sufficiently for prey populations to rebound, tigers from Russia will invade and take up residence, as will the even more endangered Amur leopard."

One evening in Vladivostok, we dined at the apartment of Dimitri Pikunov. A blue-eyed, chesty, and engaging man fairly bursting his shirt with life energy and self-celebration,

Pikunov boasted that all the raw materials for our feast—elk meat and salmon, cabbage and potatoes, mushrooms and berries, ferns and honey—had been hunted and gathered and fished and grown and prepared by himself and his attractive wife and daughters. "In America you talk a lot about appreciating the environment, but here we practice what we preach," Pikunov assured us as he poured the vodka.

Dimitri Pikunov

Displaying pictures of the tiger killed at the Vladivostok trolley stop in 1986, which showed throngs of men congratulating the excited shooter, our host let it be known that "Dima" Pikunov had been the man first summoned by the authorities to track and execute that animal. "Yes, I tracked it for them," he confided grimly, lowering his voice, "but I would not kill it. Pikunov refused to kill a tiger."

Our host told us that on January 22—the bitter cold day we had heard the tale of Sergei Denisov at Melnichnoye—a tiger had attacked and mauled a woman who was following her husband through the forest toward a rural train station outside the town of Partisansk, north of this city. When it leapt upon her after he went by, her husband ran back and attacked it bravely, bashing it with his flashlight as he yelled at her to flee; it seized and killed him as his wife ran off. A few hours later—having fed on the man's entrails and rib cage—this tiger (a male) was tracked and killed by hunters and militia. The widow reported that the tiger had been limping, a debilitating injury for a hunting animal which might well have driven it to an attack.

At the end of the evening, Olga Pikunov brought wood stools into

Hornocker and Pikunov with Udege hunters

the foyer, where, in ancient custom, we sat for a moment of silent appreciation of our evening together. Then our host escorted us through the night streets in search of a cab to take us to our hotel. In the anarchic new Russia, the Vladivostok streets are perilous at night. A few weeks earlier, our friend Igor Nikolaev, passing three idle men, had been knocked down and kicked for no good reason. Even Dersu, who had survived a mauling by a tiger and had always expected that Amba would appear one day to put an end to him, was attacked instead by brigands in Khabarovsk who robbed and murdered him.

In February 1996, Dr. Pikunov organized a range-wide census, in which an army of some 600 trackers scattered throughout the Sikhote-Alin recorded all and any pugmarks in the snow—the most comprehensive tiger census ever made, Howard Quigley said. The results were announced in November of that year after many months of analysis of the data, carefully supervised by Dale Miquelle. An estimated population of 350 adults—give or take thirty or forty—was accompanied by about a hundred juveniles and sub-adults. (Ordinarily, young animals aren't counted, since only about half of them survive.)

The final rough estimate of 450 individuals was comparable to the highest tiger population of the mid-1980s, when it was first hoped that *P. t. altaica* might be saved. "Those animals took an awful hammering in the early nineties," Howard told me happily over the telephone, "but given a little breathing room, tigers know how to survive." In his opinion, a population that includes fifty female tigers which regularly use the proposed network of semi-protected areas is needed to prevent inbreeding; 500 tigers overall might ensure a secure future for the Amur race.

Unfortunately, the good news about the tiger census had not been well received throughout the region. As Evgeny Smirnov commented, "Those who hate tiger (there are many) will rush for killing the 'extra' tigers [for] a few thousand dollars, or write to various . . . institutions that it is dangerous to live near tiger." Reminding his fellow citizens that in the Sikhote-Alin and Lazovski Reserves, where tigers were most common, there had been no case of a tiger attack on a human being in more than sixty years, and promising that any dangerous tiger would be killed to spare other tigers from retaliation, Smirnov concluded, "I'm not trying to reassure anybody, only making report on the last tiger census, saying again the old motto of real taiga men, 'Ussuri without tiger is like food without salt—just diet food.' "

In the early winter of 1997, about a year after my visit, a tiger in the Maksimovka drainage about one hundred miles north of the reserve "killed and ate hunter A. Kulikov," according to Smirnov, who visited the scene. "All found there was a rifle, a cartridge belt, parts of the clothing, the hunter's skull, and leg in the high boot." A villager reported having seen a tiger limping badly, with what seemed to be a steel trap affixed to a front paw, and geologists working not far away had seen Kulikov's dog being chased by "a big skinny tiger with abnormal bulky right fore leg . . . [Probably] the tiger had been crippled. When and by whom? There is no answer. People who knew Kulikov tell that he had promised them to fetch a tiger skin. Now his comrade regrets: 'He shouldn't have.' "

On November 12, at the same place, the crippled tiger killed a second hunter, V. Zabrovsky. "It was . . . getting dark when he walked unarmed for his rifle hidden in the old tree trunk 130 feet from the shed where his companion [awaited] him. The dog began barking, the horse neighed, and his comrade shot blindly . . . in the air, conscious of the tragedy although not seeing it." Both bodies were fed upon. Despite its condition, the tiger left the area, and the Amba tracking team finally gave up, Miquelle related, "due to 'lack of suitable transportation' (or to put it another way, because the tiger had traveled so far from the village). This animal was never heard from again, and it's my suspicion that it died that winter, unable to hunt suitable prey."

Subsequently, no other hunters dared to go there, although two hunters and five tigers had lived there peaceably last year and "didn't interfere with each other," Smirnov reported. "Hunters and tigers had nor fear either doubts. The tiger tracks could be met every day, sometimes tigers were seen visually." Though dogs were missing

from some shacks—sometimes as many as nine in a season—this was expected and it caused no panic. "Hunters in Maksimovka lived side by side with tigers that did not assault people."

In the past quarter century, human fatalities caused by tigers had been very rare in Russia, with only six cases of unprovoked attack leading to man-eating (and only one known instance since 1980, in which the same tiger took two or more people; unlike *tigris, altaica* rarely becomes a confirmed "man-eater"). Provoked attacks, on the other hand, were not uncommon. Within the few weeks following my departure, two more human deaths were the direct consequence of botched attempts to poach a tiger. Unlike the unprovoked fatalities near Melnichnoye and Partisansk, these came about when the hunters stalked and fired at the tigers, which had turned and killed them. One tiger did not even bite the poacher but simply swatted him to the ground with a paw to the head, then ran away; apparently the man had died of shock and cold.

So many deaths in a brief period was most unusual in this sparsely inhabited forest region, but a peculiar pattern of increased human mortalities in a time of drastically diminished tiger populations has been noted elsewhere in the tiger range countries, where the absence of sufficient prey may have led to increased dispersal of sub-adult animals into regions closer to human settlement. Perhaps the timing of these deaths was no more than coincidence, yet there seems little doubt that the deterioration of tiger habitat caused by timbering and mining and the epidemic poaching, not only of tigers but of their prey, has forced the hungry animals to roam farther and hunt harder, increasing the chances of conflict with human beings. Intensive hunting of game animals required by the tiger might well

have been a critical factor in these cases, and hunting for the table was unlikely to stop in this era of hard times in the new Russia. Competition with tigers for this food, not to speak of mounting human mortalities, could only lead to outcry and condemnation of the tiger, eroding the public support that will surely be critical for its survival.

A paradox still poorly understood is not why tigers attack human beings but why they do not attack more often, all the more so now that the senses and agility of *Homo sapiens*—always rudimentary when compared to those of other mammals—have been further dulled and softened by modern life. No matter how athletic and alert, a man or a woman inevitably presents a large, slow, easy prey to a hunting tiger. Thus it is curious that in all of the attacks cited above, the victims seem to fall into two categories: the tiger responded to a direct attack which probably injured it, or the tiger, previously injured, had become so incapacitated that it was unable to catch anything else—or anything *better*, as it might well seem to the frustrated tiger, to judge from how uncommon these attacks have been in relation to the opportunities. One may suppose that tigers simply dislike the smell and taste of us, as appears to be the case with the grizzly bear.

In February 1996, returning home to the United States, I found a letter from Dale Miquelle, who reported that Katia's litter—a single cub—had been confirmed. However, her next kill had been made even closer to the road—only 160 feet—so close that she could be observed on the carcass from the road shoulder. And this road habit may have been the death of her, for although she was seen traveling with her cub early in 1997, her signal went dead soon after that, and it was assumed she had been taken by a poacher. Since then, marked tigers have continued to disappear, including "Marijuana" and Geny, erstwhile mate of Katia and Natasha, and most recently Natasha herself, old #3, killed in July 1999 (her radio collar was retrieved). Both Katia and Natasha were accompanied by cubs—six altogether—which were too young to survive in the wild.

On December 12, 1998, a hunter followed tracks of a wild boar up a snowy slope above the Sheptoon River—the region where, two years before, I had seen the tigress Nadia bound across the sun-shined snow toward that great spruce. Nearing the crest, the hunter found the fresh prints of a tigress with three juveniles which appeared to be tracking the same boar. Following these tracks over the ridge, he came upon the tigers on the kill. At this point (or so he related), the tigress charged him, obliging him to shoot and kill her in self-defense. (Since it was determined that the marksman was only fifteen yards away when he first fired, one has to suspect that the tigress had not charged but had only risen from the kill, snarling a warning.) Two days later, when her radio signal became inactive, John Goodrich trekked out to the place with Volodya Velichko and Boris Litvinov of Operation Amba; they found the boar hide and the tiger carcass with most of the meat stripped off and cached under the snow. The tiger skin, dug up ten yards away, was missing whiskers and the tail tip, apparently taken as souvenirs or trophies. Departing, the man had flung the radio collar down the hillside a half mile away.

Some weeks later, after an investigation by the Amba team, the poacher was arrested and interrogated. Though he claimed self-defense, it seemed suspicious that he had risked trailing a tigress with cubs unless he intended to shoot them; tried and found guilty, he was let off with a small fine.

As for the cubs, which had been born in June, they were too

young to survive on their own and too old to adapt well to captivity, apart from being more valuable in the forest. For these reasons—and also because modern zoos dislike giving the impression that they are taking endangered animals from the wild—there seemed no point in capturing the orphaned cubs. Unlike Lena's helpless kittens, these juveniles were nearly six months old, well past the point of easy accommodation to captivity. In an attempt to tide them over the winter, special licenses were issued to permit shooting game for them, and to bring them dead animals confiscated from illegal hunters. The first time this was done, the cubs' most likely father, Dale the Bear-eater, made off with some of the meat, and the cubs followed him about a mile and a half as if trying to retrieve it. Nonetheless, all three took food throughout the winter.

The next plan was to capture and radio-collar them for the monitoring program, but by the time that permit came through, the snow had melted and the cubs had left the site. At less than a year, they were nowhere near the usual dispersal age, yet they seemed to be fending for themselves. Badger and raccoon dog, Dale thinks, were their most likely prey, with newborn ungulates coming along in warmer weather; if the juveniles survived the summer bear season, they would have a chance.

The killed tigress, of course, had been Nadia, the first wild tiger I had ever seen. It was sickening to realize that the three tigers I had felt most close to—Lena, Nadia, and Katia—had all been poached and violently destroyed.

There was good news, too. In this summer of 1999, the indomitable Tiger #1, despite the timber cutting just north of her territory, produced her third litter since her capture seven years ago; she has never left her natal territory across the river from Terney, near the sea. So far as Howard Quigley knows, Olga has been monitored longer than any other tiger ever studied.

In the early spring of 1996, I went to the zoo in Indianapolis to pay my respects to a young Amur tiger, which I found stretched gracefully on a sunny ledge, the highest and most hidden point in the outside enclosure she shares with two other *altaica*, a young female and an adult male. She peered at me—or rather, past me—through the slanted ellipses of gold-amber eyes, in the oblique and indifferent manner of all felines. Unlike her companions—and unlike most zoo tigers—this young tigress had been born in the wild, and as it happened, I had recently returned from southeastern Siberia, where I had visited the alder wood on a snowy ridge above the Kunalaika Valley on which she was captured in November 1992 as an unweaned, orphaned cub. Three years earlier, in June, I had listened intently for her mother where Lena lay beside a stream in the fresh woodlands of the Kunalaika, and so I felt a peculiar bond of place and history with this pretty creature.

According to her keepers, who were glad to hear such a close description of her home territory, the young tigress remained wary around strangers, owing to the traumatic circumstances of her capture; the zoo-bred tigress, more gregarious, had been placed in her enclosure as a "surrogate sibling" to help acclimate her to captivity and ease her nerves. At about 240 pounds, the wild tigress was beautiful and healthy, and also exceptionally valuable, due to her genes, which promised a precious infusion of new blood into captive-tiger-breeding programs all over the country—a store of genetic material that might conceivably offset some catastrophe in the precarious wild population.

Lena's daughter was on birth control medication, pending the day she would be bred by a suitable male—a male, that is, whose genes were not already widespread in American zoo populations, and could therefore offer the best match to avoid inbreeding. Of course, her cubs would be exponentially more valuable in maintaining the Amur tiger population in the wild, but that is not her story.

In 1997, this young animal would lose her firstborn cub, a common event among young tigresses in captivity as well as in the wild. In October 1998, she produced a second litter, and when I visited her in mid-November, both of her two cubs were doing fine. However, she had never recovered from her bad experience in Siberia—the noisy destruction of her mother, her own scaring capture, or both—for she became agitated in the presence of human males and was tranquil only around keeper Lynn Villers, who had taken care of her since her arrival three years before. While her cubs were still small and vulnerable, no man could so much as peer into her enclosure. The enclosure was indoors behind the exhibit pens, where a monitor provided a clear look at the family.

Lena's windowless enclosure adjoined the cage of Dzinghis, the male parent. Because he might upset or harm the mother or the cubs, Dzinghis had no access to them either, though an open panel low in the wall permitted the tiger family to sniff at one another through the bars. While I was admiring the big male, pacing relentlessly around his cage, both cubs suddenly appeared at the open panel, growling and spitting boisterously at their father, and soon their mother's wide-eyed wary face appeared behind them, peering at the human being, then at Dzinghis, who paid no attention. She still looked young, a pretty Amur tiger—all "creative fire and light," in Blake's splendorous phrase.

I have never forgotten that groan of assent at Melnichnoye when I inquired whether folks would be relieved if the tiger were exterminated, followed swiftly by loud protest to the contrary. As Sergei Zinoviev had blurted out—groping for words that might convey this access of emotion—the forest would be "boring" without tigers, by which I had supposed he meant it would lack mystery. At first I dismissed this as vainglory, yet the others all agreed. The tiger is "the soul of India," as my friends in Delhi put it, and it is the soul of Dersu's country, too.

In arguing for heroic efforts on behalf of tigers, one could cite the critical importance of biodiversity as well as the interdependence of all life. Howard Quigley reminds me, for example, how many attributes of its prey species—the astonishing alertness and keen senses, speed, and strength of the deer and boar—might never have evolved without the tensions imposed on their ecology by this great predator. But finally these abstractions seem less vital than our instinct that the aura of a creature as splendid as any on our earth, infusing man's life with myth and power and beauty, could be struck from our experience of creation only at a dreadful cost. "Life would be *less* without the tiger," Howard has observed, and I agree.

One cannot speak for those who live in tiger country, but the vivid

presence of Hu Lin, the King—merely knowing that His Lordship is out there in the forest—brings me deep happiness. That winter afternoon in the Kunalaika, the low sunlight in the south glancing off black silhouetted ridges and shattered into frozen blades by the black trees, the ringing clarity of the great cat tracks on the snow-glazed ice, the blood trace and stark signs of the elk's passage—that was pure joy.

NOTES

About measurements: For simplicity's sake, U.S. units of measurement are used throughout the text. To convert to metric, use the following formulas: 1 inch = 2.54 centimeters; 1 foot = .305 meter; 1 acre = .405 hectare; 1 mile = 1.609 kilometers; 1 square mile = 2.589 square kilometers; 1 pound = .454 kilogram. To convert degrees Fahrenheit to degrees Celsius, subtract 32 degrees and divide by 1.8.

5. "On a tree nearby": Vladimir K. Arseniev, *Dersu the Trapper* (New York: Dutton, 1941).

14. " 'The Tiger Is God' ": Nicholas Courtney, *Tiger: Symbol of Freedom* (London: Quartet, 1980).

22. *The Ecology of the Amur Tiger*: Igor Nikolaev and A. G. Yudakov, *The Ecology of the Amur Tiger* (Moscow: 1987).

25. "there are also accounts": Arthur Sowerby, in *The Naturalist in Manchuria*, as quoted in Vratislav Mazak, "Notes on the Siberian Long-Haired Tiger," *Mammalia* (1967) 1:537–73.

27. "Besides excellent hearing . . . wind-danced leaves": Tiger, lion, leopard, and cheetah could all inhabit the same regions of India not only because their ecological niches were quite different but because their recognition markings or lack of them were barriers to hybridization when their paths crossed. (It is not a coincidence that in both pairs of similarly patterned or unpatterned species—lion and mountain lion, leopard and jaguar—the members of each pair live widely separated on different continents.) See N. A. Neff, *The Big Cats* (New York: Harry N. Abrams, 1982), p. 22.

33. "With support from . . . environmental organizations": These included Russia's Socio-Ecological Union—the SEU—and the United States' Pacific Environmental Resource Council.

34. " 'The high officials . . . they have not' ": Alexei Grigoriev, address to zapovednik conference at Bolshe Khetskhir, June 1992.

41. " 'Molecular phylogenies . . . lion, leopard, and jaguar' ": Andrew Kitchener, "Biogeographical Change and Subspeciation in the Tiger," in *Riding the Tiger*, edited by John Seidensticker, Sarah Christie, and Peter Jackson (London: Cambridge University Press, 1999).

42. " 'There is reason . . . in search of food' ": N. A. Baikov, *Big Game Hunting in Manchuria* (London: Hutchinson, 1936), p. 186. See also Neff, *The Big Cats*, p. 137.

42. "theory that *Panthera tigris* originated in southern China": Sandra Herrington, "Subspecies and the Conservation of *Panthera tigris*," in *Tigers of the World*, edited by Ronald L. Tilson and Ulysses S. Seal (Park Ridge, N.J.: Noyes Publications, 1987).

42. "identical . . . except for size": In the full skeletons, the lion's leg bone is marginally longer.

42. " 'It is commonly stated . . . eastern Asia' ": Vratislav Mazak, "*Panthera tigris*," *Mammalian Species* 152 (May 8, 1981), pp. 1–8; Hemmer, "The Phylogeny of the Tiger," and Herrington, "Subspecies," in *Tigers of the World*.

44. "Sakhalin Island and Japan and Borneo": John Seidensticker, conversations with the author, 1995–99.

44. "icon and a subject of Japanese art": See D. T. Suzuki, *Zen and Japanese Culture* (Princeton, N.J.: Princeton University Press, 1993).

47. "largest of the modern tigers": A male Siberian on a game farm in Canada is said to weigh over one thousand pounds—a half-ton tiger!—

even though zoo flab weighs much less than hunting muscle; if this creature exists, it is surely the largest cat of any species ever recorded.

47. "At least one authority": conversations with John Seidensticker, 1995–99.

50. " 'No doubt . . . extinction' ": Francis Harper, *Extinct and Vanishing Mammals of the Old World* (New York: New York Zoological Park, 1945).

51. "the farthest east-west outposts": "Across the range of any species, individuals at the outermost fringes display a unique set of adaptations, and if protected will increase the genetic diversity across the species range more so than the subspecies near the center of distribution. The Far Eastern leopard is a shining example . . . related closely only to its nearest neighbor, the northern Chinese leopard, which may be extinct in the wild." John Seidensticker, cited by Dale Miquelle in *Zoogoer*, September/October 1998.

53. " 'The small species' ": Bassett Digby, "The Ways of Northern Tigers," in *Tigers, Gold and Witch-doctors* (New York: Harcourt Brace, 1928).

53. " 'poisoned bait' ": Richard Perry, *The World of the Tiger*, quoted in *The Soul of the Tiger*, by Jeffrey A. McNeely and Paul S. Wachtel (New York: Doubleday, 1988).

53. " 'In Baku' ": Fitzroy Maclean, *To Caucasus, the End of the Earth* (London: Jonathan Cape, 1976), p. 192.

54. "an American researcher": See Paul Joslin abstract, "Status of the Caspian Tiger in Iran," in *Cats of the World*," by S. D. Miller and D. D. Everett (National Wildlife Federation, 1982).

54. "distinguishable from the Amur race": *altaica*, subspecific trinomial for the Amur tiger chosen by C. J. Temminck in 1844, refers to the Altai or Pisihan Mountains of Korea, not the Altai of Mongolia; see Mazak, "*Panthera tigris.*"

55. " 'Manchurian' tigers in the mountains of northeastern China": Ma Yiqing, "The Manchurian Tiger in China," in *Wildlife Conservation Management* (Harbin, China, 1979).

56. "North Korea's recent claim": Chris Dobson, *South China Morning Post*, May 17, 1995.

56. "a recent report": "A Survey of Tigers and Prey Resources in the Paektusan Area, Lyangan Province, North Korea, Winter 1998," conducted by the Korean People's Democratic Republic Academy of Science Institute

of Geography and sponsored by WCS (the Wildlife Conservation Society of New York).

57. "It is said to be": Neff, *The Big Cats*.

58. " 'the tiger is now extremely scarce' ": Lu Houji and Sheng Helin, Red Data Book, Convention on International Trade in Endangered Species, 1972.

58. "the tiger's range was now essentially restricted": National Geographic Society map notes based on data provided by Wang Sung, director of the Mammals of China Project at Academia Sinica.

59. "The most recent subspecies": Vratislav Mazak, "New Tiger Subspecies from Southeast Asia," *Mammalia* 32 (1968):1.

59. "It is said to have": Neff, *The Big Cats*.

60. "one writer cites": Ibid.

60. "known to resort to carrion": "The Siberian tiger has a ghoulish trick of digging up graves, and in many villages between Vladivostok and Korea an old man is appointed watchman of the cemetery, where he sits with a gun in a stoutly built little log hut, from dusk to dawn." From Digby, *Tigers, Gold and Witch-doctors*.

61. "According to Rabinowitz": See Alan Rabinowitz, "Estimating the Indochinese Tiger Population in Thailand," *Biological Conservation* 65 (1993), pp. 213–17.

62. "As wildlife biologist George Schaller . . . Rabinowitz agrees": Ibid.

63. " 'the trans-boundary tiger populations' ": J. L. D. Smith et al., "Metapopulation Structure of Tigers in Thailand," in *Riding the Tiger*, p. 174.

64. " 'a comprehensive survey' ": Conducted by an American group called Cat Action Treasury, or CAT.

64. " 'Despite thirty years' ": Michael Sheridan and Tom Fawthrop, "Tigers Roar Back in the Jungles of Cambodia," *The London Sunday Times*, April 25, 1999.

65. " 'The tiger dies' ": Neil Franklin et al., "Last of the Indonesian Tigers: A Cause for Optimism," *Riding the Tiger*, p. 144.

65. "In former times . . . rest in peace": McNeely and Wachtel, *Soul of the Tiger*.

65–66. "Farther south . . . between the islands": John Seidensticker, conversations with the author.

67. " 'Fearing [that] the tiger is a spirit' ": Mochtar Lubis, *Harimau! Harimau!* (Jakarta: Eureka, 1991).

68. " 'about thirty-five professional Indonesian' ": R. L. Tilson et al., *Sumatran Tiger: Population and Habitat Viability Analysis Report* (Apple Valley, MN: Indonesian Forest Protection and Nature Conservation and JUCNISSC Captive Breeding Specialist Group, 1992).

69. "a subsequent report": Sumatran Tiger Report, 1992. See also World Wildlife Fund–U.S. and Wildlife Conservation Society, "A Framework for Identifying High Priority Areas and Actions for the Conservation of Tigers in the Wild" by Neil Franklin, 1997.

69. "the tigers in Way Kambas": *Wildlife Society Bulletin*, 1997.

71. "It is said . . . through their nostrils": Stephen Harrigan, "The Tiger Is God," originally published as "The Nature of the Beast," *Texas Monthly*, July 1988.

73. "As late as 1968 . . . in the 1970s": John Seidensticker, "Bearing Witness: Observations on the Extinction of *P. t. balica* and *P. t. sondaica*," in *Tigers of the World*, ed. Tilson and Seal, pp. 1–8, 34.

73. " 'Meru-Betiri and the Javan tiger' ": Julius Tahija, quoted in McNeely and Wachtel, *Soul of the Tiger*, p. 197.

78. "Since these wanderers kill": Valmik Thapar, *Land of the Tiger* (Berkeley: University of California Press, 1998).

78. "some 400 tigers": Neff, *The Big Cats*.

79. "*Bagh! Bagh!*": Conversation with Fateh Singh at Ranthambhore, 1992.

83. " 'do not show themselves' ": Conversation at Delhi, February 1996.

85. " 'there were more tigers at Kanha' ": George B. Schaller, *The Deer and the Tiger* (Chicago: University of Chicago Press, 1967).

88. "may be doomed": "The tiger's future in the Sundarbans, as in the Russian Far East, lies in identifying and protecting and linking areas that will support fifty or more reproducing females," John Seidensticker comments. One of the lessons of the Siberian Tiger Project, he notes, has been to demonstrate how radio telemetry, combined with foot surveys and the new mapping techniques, can more clearly establish what tigers really need so that long-term-use plans can be shaped accordingly. Similarly, a new plan for Bhutan makes use of such data to link regions in a network of habitat that should sustain about fifty females. Rather than continuing a discussion about how many tigers there are in the Sundarbans, he suggests, "we should be identifying these critical areas."

88. "this extended study": The study has been led by Drs. Hemanta Mishra (who was close to the King and therefore critical to the success of the

whole project) and Mel Sunquist, then Dr. James L. D. Smith, all of them assisted by Charles McDougal, who is still in Chitwan as a Smithsonian research associate.

90.   " 'I think tigers . . . as lions do' ": Thapar, *Land of the Tiger*.

90.   " 'Seidensticker's work has shown' ": Alan Rabinowitz, unpublished notes and conversation with the author, August 10, 1999.

92.   "One published report": Ramachandra Gupta, "The Authoritarian Biologist and the Arrogance of Anti-Humanism: Wildlife Conservation in the Third World," *The Ecologist*, January/February 1997. "That's what his friend told him," says Ullas Karanth, who knows Gupta, "but that's not what was said. I know, because I was there and he was not."

92.   "Karanth himself has expressed regret": Ullas Karanth, "Long-Term Monitoring of Tigers: Lessons from Nagarahole," in *Riding the Tiger*, p. 116.

92.   "reports appeared in *The Guardian*": Adrian Levy et al., "Save the Rhino but Kill the People," *The Guardian Weekly*, March 30, 1997. Also, unpublished letter to Georgina Henry, Deputy Editor, Guardian Newspapers, from John G. Robinson, Vice President for International Conservation, WCS, and Joshua Ginsberg, Director, WCS Asia Program, June 1997.

94.   " 'After all . . . sustainable use of resources' ": Dale Miquelle, letters and conversations, July 1999.

97.   "a *Time* story": "Tigers on the Brink," *Time* 143 (March 28, 1994).

97.   "Kumar and Wright are in agreement": Ashok Kumar and Belinda Wright, "Combatting Tiger Poaching and Illegal Wildlife Trade in India," in *Riding the Tiger*, p. 243.

97.   "every last one had been set free": A first conviction and imprisonment was finally won in 1999.

98.   "a recent analysis by scientists at the National Cancer Institute": Joelle Wentzel et al., "Subspecies of Tigers; Molecular Assessment Using 'Voucher Specimens' of Geographically Traceable Individuals," in *Riding the Tiger*, p. 42.

98.   "Kitchener's morphological review": Andrew Kitchener et al., "Tiger Distribution: Phenotypic Variation and Conservation Issues," in *Riding the Tiger*, p. 19.

99.   "In a recent paper": John Seidensticker, "Bearing Witness: Observations

on the Extinction of *Panthera tigris balica* and *Panthera tigris sondaica.* In *Tigers of the World*, pp. 1–8.

100. "an article that appeared": Joel Cracraft et al., "Sorting Out Tigers: *Panthera tigris*, Mitochondrial Sequences, Nuclear Inserts, Systematics, and Conservation Genetics," *Animal Conservation* 1 (1998), pp. 139–50.

102. "John Seidensticker agrees": Conversations with the author, Washington, D.C., June–August 1999.

104. " 'looking for [his] home' ": In July 1999 Dale Miquelle married his Russian fiancée on a U.S. visit, before returning to Siberia.

114. "bear gallbladders": Hyundai's elderly ex-president, Mr. Jung Ju Young, has attributed his excellent health to a branch of his company—presumably the Bikin River operation mentioned earlier—that keeps him supplied with bile from bear gallbladders, which are worth $2,000 apiece or more to wildlife poachers. Mr. Jung declared cheerfully that he consumed bear bile "all the time."

114. "between 1975 and 1992 . . . that year alone": According to WWF International's wildlife monitoring arm (called TRAFFIC), which has researched most of these figures; correspondence from Ginette Hemley, WWF-U.S., and Kristin Nowell, a consultant to WWF and TRAFFIC.

114. "Before 1992 . . . dried bones": *Cat News*, September 1993.

114. "In the next few years . . . from 1990 to 1994": Michael Specter, *The New York Times*, September 5, 1995.

115. "a national decree": Entitled "On Saving the Amur Tiger and Other Endangered Flora and Fauna of the Russian Far East."

116. "an illegal tiger-wine manufacturer": Michael Day, *Fight for the Tiger* (London: Headline Books, 1995).

116. "relying for support . . . eat chickens": Dale Miquelle, note to the author, July 1999.

119. "Tiger density": M. E. Sunquist, "The Social Organization of Tigers in Royal Chitwan National Park, Nepal," *Smithsonian Contributions to Zoology* (Washington, D.C.: Smithsonian Institution Press, 1981), pp. 1–98.

124. "financial support for anti-poaching measures": Six of the reserve's armed forest rangers were being paid by Germany's World Wildlife Federation, with additional support from Russia's Mezhcombank. The patrol was also sponsored by the National Geographic Society, WCS, and the National Fish and Wildlife Foundation, as well as the environmentally

challenged Exxon Corporation, which in its heroic efforts to "green" its image, was naturally claiming the tiger's share of the credit: "Exxon is committed to tiger conservation," intoned an Exxon press release in 1995. "Over $5 million has been given by our companies to support key projects. These beautiful animals must not be allowed to disappear." Exxon could part with these sums without a wince since, as of the spring of 1999, it had not paid out a single cent of the $5.3 billion it was fined in court for the Valdez oil disaster almost a decade earlier, and accumulates $800 million interest every year on that $5 billion it owes its pollution victims but will not pay. ("Based upon its experience in this case," as the presiding judge observed a few years ago, "this court is concerned that Exxon's litigators will be asked to devise any possible procedural roadblock to defer payment.") See *Amicus Journal*, Summer 1999.

158. "the creature is even closer to extinction": The Amur or Far Eastern leopard, *Panthera pardus orientalis*, is now confined to the common borderlands between the Russian Far East, China, and North Korea, in the Eastern Manchurian Mountains region surrounding the Tunen River drainage—"some of the least favorable habitat in its former range, where deep snows and long winters create poor conditions for an animal normally associated with African woodlands and the Asian tropics" (Dale Miquelle, in *Zoogoer*, September/October 1998). Like the North China race of Asian leopard, *orientalis* may already be extinct in China and the Koreas (though rumored to persist in the DMZ); perhaps forty are left in southwestern Primorski Krai. Unlike the Amur tiger, *P. p. orientalis* is precariously rare even in captivity.

160. "a survey in the winter of 1999": Dale Miquelle, notes and conversation, July 1999.

161. "this tiger . . . was tracked": Since then, Olga's sub-adult male cub had been destroyed after trying to stalk a forest ranger at a reserve cabin—unsuccessfully, being weak and very thin, due to an internal injury which had starved it.

162. "a range-wide census": With certain restrictions, a tiger's sex and age can be determined from its print, but due to the wide variability of these pugmarks under differing conditions in the wild, they are no longer considered a reliable gauge by Ullas Karanth, who says that when "rigorously tested," census trackers in India were unable to distinguish tigers consistently on the basis of their tracks. Using "camera traps"—the au-

tomatic camera is set off when a tiger crosses its beam—to record the unique striping pattern of each tiger, he discovered that there were sixty-five tigers in his research area at Nagarahole rather than the previously estimated forty. (He continues to believe, however, that pugmark counts reported from the Sundarbans are generally too high.) In addition, Karanth makes rough prey counts, the better to judge the capacity of a given area to support tigers.

163. " 'Those who hate . . . diet food' ": Evgeny Smirnov, *Terney News*, January 15, 1997.

164. "On November 12": Dale Miquelle, correspondence with the author, August 12, 1999.

167. "One may suppose": C. McDougal, The Man-eating Tiger in Geographical and Historical Perspective," in *Tigers of the World*, ed. Tilson and Seal, pp. 435–48.